A FIELD GUIDE TO

BIRDS

OF THE BIG BEND

A FIELD GUIDE TO BIRDS OF THE BIG BEND

NEW, REVISED EDITION

BY ROLAND H. WAUER

ILLUSTRATIONS BY NANCY MCGOWAN

Illustrations copyright © 1985 by Nancy McGowan.

Copyright © 1985 by Big Bend Natural History Association, Inc. All rights including reproduction by photographic or electronic process and translation into other languages are fully reserved under the International Copyright Union, the Universal Copyright Convention, and the Pan-American Copyright Convention. Reproduction or use of this book in whole or in part in any manner without written permission of the publisher is strictly prohibited.

Texas Monthly Press, Inc.
P.O. Box 1569
Austin, Texas 78767

A B C D E F G H

Library of Congress Cataloging in Publication Data

Wauer, Roland H.
A field guide to birds of the Big Bend.

Includes index.
1. Birds—Texas—Big Bend National Park—Identification. 2. Big Bend National Park. (Tex.) I. Title.
QL684.T4W39 1985 598.29764'932 85-9744
ISBN 0-87719-027-5
ISBN 0-87719-010-0 (pbk.)

Contents

Introduction

The Big Bend Country is one of those special "must visit" places for birders. It is one of a handful of localities in the southern latitudes of the United States that represent quality birding. Places like the Everglades, Aransas, Santa Ana, Ramsey Canyon, the Chiricahuas, and the Chisos sooner or later show up on every birder's calendar. Big Bend National Park offers a wider variety of birds—425 species have been recorded—than any other national park.

Thc intcnt of this book is to hclp thc Big Bcnd visitor find thc particular birds he or she may want to see. It is a where-to-go-to-find-what-book, not an identification guide. *A Field Guide to Birds of the Big Bend* should be a companion to the popular identification handbooks that more than likely are already part of your library.

This book was written to satisfy two worlds: that of the ornithologist, who may be most interested in statistics and records, and that of the birder, who may watch birds simply for the sheer thrill of seeing an old friend or making a new one.

The first edition of *Birds of Big Bend National Park and Vicinity* appeared in 1973. It contained an annotated list of 385 species of birds; 359 of those were included in the regular list of "accepted" species, and 26 were listed as hypothetical in a list of "uncertain" species. This revised edition contains 425 species, an addition of 40 species, 373 of which are included on the accepted list, and 52 of which are listed as "Birds of Uncertain Occurrence."

Two hundred six of the 359 accepted species required some text changes; a tremendous amount of new information has been accumulated on Big Bend birds since 1973. Only 107 species required no changes at all in the texts or common and taxonomic names. (When no records later than the early 1970s are listed, it should not be assumed that there have been no new sightings, particularly if the bird is a common one. The earlier records continue to be representative.)

Most interesting are the new discoveries that have become part of the accepted species list. There are eleven of these: Ross' Goose, Wild Turkey, Forster's Tern, Varied Thrush, Aztec Thrush, Bendire's Thrasher, Tennessee Warbler, Bay-breasted Warbler, Kentucky Warbler, Rufous-capped Warbler, and Common Grackle. Eleven additional species were elevated from the 1973 "Birds of Uncertain Occurrence" to the new accepted species list: Black-shouldered Kite, Elegant Trogon, Rose-throated Becard, Steller's Jay, Veery, Cape May Warbler, Golden-cheeked Warbler, Yellow-throated Warbler, Red-faced Warbler, Purple Finch, and Evening Grosbeak.

The list of uncertain occurrences has changed considerably. Only 16 species remain from the earlier list, but 35 were added. These birds are not sufficiently documented, in my mind, to be included with those fully documented and/or acceptable species listed above. Many represent very tentative records, while others will undoubtedly be moved into accepted status when there are additional sightings or more scientific documentation by either a photograph or a specimen.

Additional changes were required because of the publication of the sixth edition of the American Ornithologists' Union's *Check-list of North American Birds* (1983). The AOU is responsible for all changes in common and taxonomic names of North American birds, and every five to ten years, it publishes a revised list. All bird publications or revisions that follow adhere to the changes. The AOU was responsible for 49 changes in common names and 51 changes in taxonomic names of birds included in this edition of *A Field Guide to Birds of the Big Bend*. In addition to the common and taxonomic name changes, 4 of Big Bend's bird species were split into 2 separate species—Snow Goose into Snow and Ross' Goose, Screech Owl into Eastern and Western Screech-Owls, Traill's Flycatcher into Willow and Alder Flycatchers, and Tropical Kingbird into Tropical and Couch's Kingbirds—and 15 of the 1973 list of species were lumped into 7 species: Mallard and Mexican Duck are now Mallard; Yellow-shafted and Red-shafted Flickers are now Northern Flicker; House and Brown-throated Wrens are now House Wren; Red-eyed and Yellow-green Vireos are now Red-eyed Vireo; Myrtle and Audubon's Warblers are now Yellow-rumped Warbler; Slate-colored, Oregon, and Gray-headed Juncos are now Dark-eyed Junco; and Baltimore and Bullock's Orioles are now Northern Oriole. In those cases when the two forms can be separated in the field by sight alone, I have continued to discuss them separately within the appropriate "superspecies."

Fourteen of the species that were reported in the 1973 edition of this book have clearly increased in status. Since the 1973 species accounts were developed on the basis of thousands of records, some as early as 1901 by the U.S. Biological Survey, and hundreds of hours of personal observations between 1966 and 1972, these status changes are not the result of a greater number of observations since 1973. I must admit, however, that the abundant reports since the publication of the 1973 edition have tended to include more out-of-the-ordinary sightings than before. The more recent records have filled in holes of knowledge, so that this edition probably gives a clearer perspective on Big Bend's avifauna than the earlier version.

The 14 species that have increased in status since 1973 include:

Great Egret, Black-shouldered Kite, Mississippi Kite, Bald Eagle, Common Black-Hawk, Gray Hawk, Prairie Falcon, White-eared Hummingbird, Golden-fronted Woodpecker, Steller's Jay, Scrub Jay, Long-billed Thrasher, Red-faced Warbler, and Painted Redstart. The most significant feature of this list of 14 species is that 6 are raptors. Although there has been an increased awareness of the importance of raptors as indicators of environmental quality in recent years—particularly within the Big Bend Country, where the Chihuahuan Desert Research Institute biologists have been most active—and birders are therefore most apt to report these species, that cannot be the sole reason for these increases. It may relate to reported reductions in the use of biocides in the United States and adjacent Mexico, or it may suggest loss of habitats at other localities, or it may be natural and caused by a wide variety of environmental changes relating to climate or whatnot.

Whatever is causing these changes, as long as it is of natural origin, the birder to the Big Bend will benefit. It is evident that the bird life of Big Bend National Park is more interesting and exciting than it was earlier in the century and even ten years ago.

Bird Finding

Finding a maximum number of birds can usually be accomplished by visiting all the different habitats within the various plant communities. If one wishes to find particular species of birds, however, it is most profitable to search only within suitable habitats at the proper time of year. One would be extremely unlikely to find a Painted Bunting at Boot Spring in December or a Townsend's Solitaire at Rio Grande Village in July.

There are several places within the park that a birder should visit if he or she is interested in a maximum number of species. Rio Grande Village is the best place I know for consistently finding a large number of birds. The major areas to search at Rio Grande Village include the cottonwood groves behind the store to the west, the ponds next to the campground, the campground proper and the mesquite thickets just across the roadway to the north, the Rio Grande Village Nature Trail, and the adjacent desert hillsides.

The second most productive area is the Chisos Basin. This includes the drainage below the campground, the vicinity of the sewage lagoons, and the area along the Window Trail. During the six years I served as the chief park naturalist at Big Bend National Park, I made regular visits to the Basin Campground and the upper four fifths of the Window Trail, returning along the trail to where one can easily enter the Oak Creek drainage and then follow it upward past the lagoons and to a point directly below the lower loop of the campground. From there, one can return to the campground via a surfaced service road.

There are several other localities within the park where approximately the same bird species can be found. Green Gulch can sometimes be quite productive, particularly during the fall migration. Upper Blue Creek Canyon is best in spring. Lower Pine Canyon can be a good area for birds except in midsummer.

In summer, a visit to Boot Canyon is a must. Although the Colima Warbler can usually be found at Laguna Meadow, the area between Boot Spring and the South Rim can be very rewarding. One of the best localities for consistently finding highland birds, including the Colima Warbler, from April 15 to September 1 is about two hundred yards beyond the Juniper Canyon side trail. Birders who are not able to walk or ride horseback to Boot Spring can usually find most of the same birds at Laguna Meadow, which is one mile closer to the Chisos Basin. Another area that can be very good in spring, summer, and fall is the Lost Mine Trail. This trail starts at 5,600 feet in elevation and a two-mile walk offers some high-country exposure for a minimum of time.

The Lost Mine Trail, however, is never as productive, birdwise, as Boot Canyon and Laguna Meadow.

In late fall and early winter, one can hardly go wrong with a visit to Castolon. The weedy fields adjacent to the roadway to Santa Elena, Chihuahua, and along Alamo Creek can produce more sparrows than anywhere else in the park. Dugout Wells, located just below Panther Junction on the road to Rio Grande Village, can be very productive during the spring migration.

For those birders who like to find a bench and sit and wait for their feathered friends to happen by, two places are suggested: the Old Sam Nail Ranch and the Rio Grande Village Nature Trail. The nature trail has already been mentioned. The Old Sam Nail Ranch is located along the Castolon Road and is situated on Cottonwood Creek. Although the creek is dry most of the year, birds gather at the old ranch site because of the water available from a working windmill. A bench located beneath the walnuts and willow is a relaxing place to bird with a minimum of effort.

Fewer than 10 percent of Big Bend's birds are permanent residents. The majority spend only a few hours to a few months in the area as migrants, or as summer or winter residents. As a result, Big Bend's avian composition and density fluctuate considerably. The seasonal variations of bird species at Rio Grande Village (1,900 feet in elevation) and the Chisos Basin (5,400 feet in elevation) are illustrated in Figure 1, which is based upon field trips of three to five hours' duration throughout the year from August 1, 1966, to June 30, 1971. A total of 293 field trips were made to Rio Grande Village and 109 to the Chisos Basin.

The Migration

Spring can arrive early in the Big Bend. The spring migration usually begins before the end of February with the arrival of Violet-green Swallows along the Rio Grande. Black dalea and black brush acacia begin to bloom in lowland washes by early March, and their aromatic flowers may attract Lucifer and Black-chinned Hummingbirds. By mid-March, the spring migration is evident throughout the desert. Numbers of spring migrants increase gradually throughout late March, accelerate rapidly in April, and reach a peak during the last days of April and the first week of May. The high point is followed by a swift decrease in the number of species passing through the area during the rest of May and early June.

Spring migrants are far more numerous in the lowlands, particularly along the river, than in the mountains. For example, 52 species is the largest number that I have recorded at the Chisos Basin (within five hours on April 27, 1969), versus 93 at Rio Grande Village (within six hours on May 3, 1970).

As an example of what birds can be found at this maximum period, the list of 93 species recorded at Rio Grande Village is as follows:

Least Grebe
Pied-billed Grebe
American Bittern
Green-winged Teal
Blue-winged Teal
Northern Shoveler
Gadwall
American Wigeon
Black Vulture
Turkey Vulture
Sharp-shinned Hawk
Red-tailed Hawk
American Kestrel
Common Moorhen
American Coot
Killdeer
Solitary Sandpiper
Spotted Sandpiper
White-winged Dove
Mourning Dove
Inca Dove
Common Ground-Dove
Yellow-billed Cuckoo
Greater Roadrunner
Groove-billed Ani
Great Horned Owl
Lesser Nighthawk
White-throated Swift
Black-chinned Hummingbird
Ladder-backed Woodpecker
Olive-sided Flycatcher
Vermilion Flycatcher
Ash-throated Flycatcher
Western Wood-Pewee
Say's Phoebe
Western Kingbird
Violet-green Swallow
Northern Rough-winged Swallow
Cliff Swallow
Barn Swallow
Common Raven
Verdin
House Wren
Marsh Wren
Ruby-crowned Kinglet
Blue-gray Gnatcatcher
Hermit Thrush
Northern Mockingbird
Curve-billed Thrasher
Water Pipit
Cedar Waxwing
Bell's Vireo
Solitary Vireo
Warbling Vireo
Lucy's Warbler
Northern Parula
Yellow Warbler
Yellow-rumped Warbler
Townsend's Warbler
American Redstart
Northern Waterthrush
MacGillivray's Warbler
Common Yellowthroat
Hooded Warbler
Wilson's Warbler
Yellow-breasted Chat
Summer Tanager
Western Tanager
Northern Cardinal
Pyrrhuloxia
Blue Grosbeak
Indigo Bunting
Painted Bunting
Dickcissel

Black-throated Sparrow
Lincoln's Sparrow
Swamp Sparrow
White-throated Sparrow
Brewer's Blackbird
Brown-headed Cowbird
Black-vented Oriole
Orchard Oriole
Hooded Oriole
Scott's Oriole
House Finch
Lesser Goldfinch
House Sparrow

Many of the birds found at Rio Grande Village were also recorded in the Basin on April 27, 1969. The following were recorded only in the Basin:

Scaled Quail
Blue-throated Hummingbird
Acorn Woodpecker
Hammond's Flycatcher
Dusky Flycatcher
Gray Flycatcher
Gray-breasted Jay
Tufted Titmouse
Bushtit
Cactus Wren
Rock Wren
Canyon Wren
Bewick's Wren
Gray Vireo
Rufous-sided Towhee
Rufous-crowned Sparrow
Black-chinned Sparrow
Dark-eyed Junco
Pine Siskin

Fall migration in the lowlands is only a shadow of the spring movement. Although postnesting herons and shorebirds may reach the river area in mid-July, the majority of the southbound birds do not begin to increase until the end of that month. A gradual buildup continues throughout August, reaches a peak in mid-September, and drops off during October. There is a second but lighter increase during late November and the first few days of December.

Birds begin to increase in the mountains immediately after the spring migration subsides. Some after-breeding, floodplain, and desert birds move up into the mountains in June. The first of these is the Rufous Hummingbird, which may reach the mountain slopes by late July. The number of southbound migrants reaches its peak in mid-September. Movement through the mountains is heavier in fall than in spring, although it is still considerably less than along the Rio Grande.

The differences in spring and fall movements of birds through the park area may be explained in two ways. First, the northbound migration is shorter. It has a rather moderate buildup but drops off swiftly, lasting only about two months. Conversely, the southward movement is more gradual and is scattered out over three and a half months. Second, the number of birds passing through the park is lower in fall than in spring. This is due at least in part to the topography of the Big Bend Country. Spring migrants follow north-south desert valleys and ridges and are naturally funneled into the lower Big Bend along the western edge of the Sierra del Carmen, which forms the eastern edge of the park and runs south into Mexico for almost 100 miles. Fall migrants are often diverted toward the southeast by the Santiago Mountains, which form a barrier to lowland migrants just north of the park. I have watched flocks of blackbirds and individual gulls and hawks change their course to the southeast, toward Black Gap Wildlife Management Area and the eastern side of the Sierra del Carmen, as they approach the ridges just north of Persimmon Gap.

Figure 2 illustrates the relative abundance of five groups of birds that are regular migrants through the Big Bend Country. Ducks begin to move through the area during the last of February and early March. They become common along the river and at adjacent ponds from mid-March through mid-May, and stragglers continue to pass through the area until mid-June. Fall migrants are less numerous; postnesting birds may reach the Big Bend during the second week of August, but the peak of the fall movement does not occur until late September and lasts through October. Southbound waterfowl continue to pass through the area in small numbers until early November, and stragglers can usually be found along the river until late November. During very mild winters the fall migration may be only half as great as that of normal years. Late winters may result in a movement of waterfowl through the park as much as three to five weeks later.

Although the Rio Grande would seem to be a physical pathway for migrating water birds, they are never common in the Big Bend; only about twenty kinds of shorebirds have been recorded within the park. These birds do not reach the area until mid-March. They become most numerous from mid-April to early May, decreasing considerably by mid-May, and stragglers continue to move through the area until the end of that month. The Killdeer is the park's only nesting shorebird. Fall migrants reach the Big Bend quite early; Solitary, Spotted, Baird's, and Least Sandpipers may appear by mid-July. The whole southward movement extends from mid-July through early November, with a minor peak evident from August 20 to September 12.

Migrant hawks are sporadic within the Big Bend. They are usually found alone or in twos or threes; there are no waves of hawks like those that occur in the eastern part of the country. Early spring migrants arrive at the park in mid-March, a peak is reached during the last three weeks of April and early May, and stragglers continue to pass through the Big Bend until the first of June. Fall migrants begin to appear in mid-August and reach a high during late August to mid-October. Migrant hawks can usually be found until about November 12.

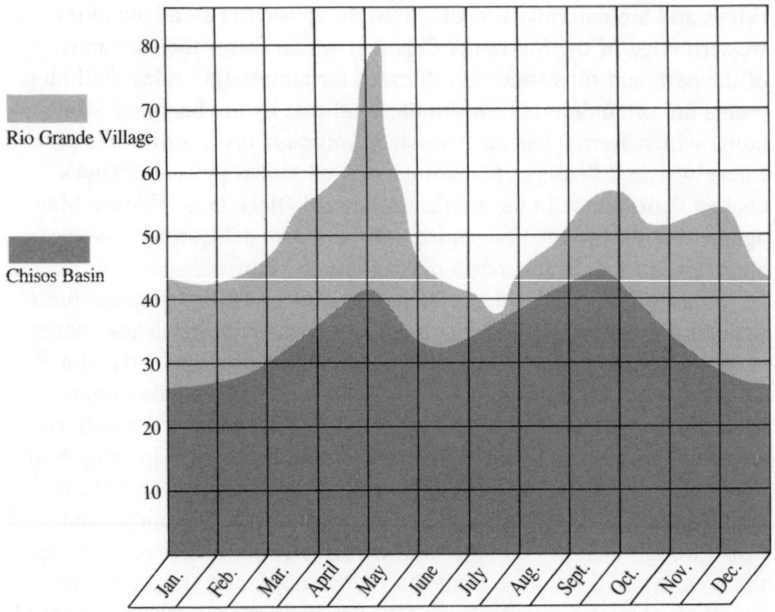

Figure 1. Seasonal variation of bird species averaged over a five-year period.

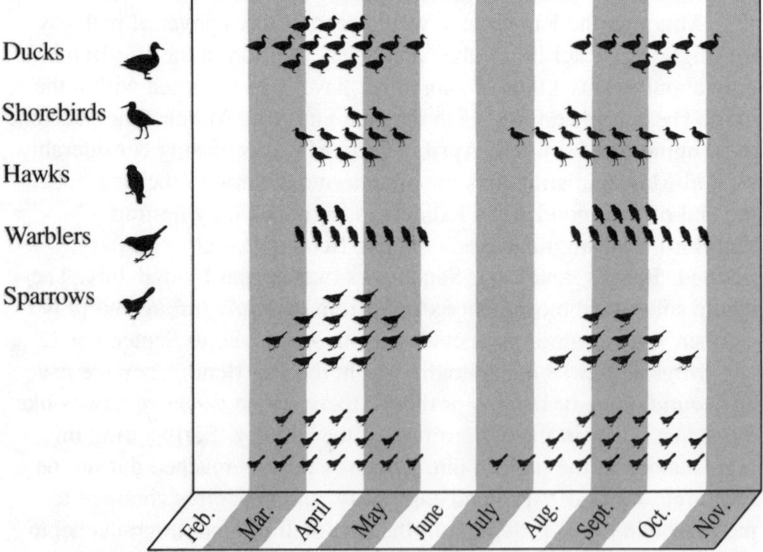

Figure 2. Relative abundance of five groups of migratory birds.

The movement of warblers through the Big Bend produces the largest numbers of birds of any single family. Some spring migrants can be found the second week of March; their numbers increase greatly during the last of April and the first half of May, and they remain fairly numerous until late May. Stragglers can usually be seen through mid-June. Some southbound Black-and-white Warblers have been recorded in early July, but most of the early fall migrants do not reach the Big Bend until the first part of August. The early birds have been found only in the mountains; lowland migrants are rarely detected until mid-August. The fall movement is not as dramatic as that in the spring, and a population peak is reached from late August through late September. Southbound birds appear throughout October, although only two or three species can usually be found by the end of the month.

The Big Bend's sporadic sparrow migration is generally restricted to the lowlands below 5,000 feet in elevation. Some movement is evident during the last days of February, but the main spring migration does not get under way until mid-March. Sparrows continue to be common migrants until late May, while stragglers can often be found until early June. Southbound Chipping and Lark Sparrows may reach the park as early as the last half of July, and Lark Buntings usually appear during the first days of August. The bulk of the southward sparrow migration does not become evident until September and lasts through October. Fall migrants continue to move through the area until late November.

The Breeding Season

More than one hundred species of birds have been found to nest within Big Bend National Park in recent years. Lowland residents are first to begin their territorial defense and to nest. Some of the desert species may be incubating before the first of April, and some mountain birds may not arrive on their breeding grounds until late April.

Nesting birds of the *floodplain* include a few permanent residents, but the majority reside within the Big Bend only during the spring and summer months. Most of these arrive in late March and April. The last of the summer residents to reach the area are the Yellow-billed Cuckoo and the Blue Grosbeak. The most conspicuous breeding birds of the floodplain include White-winged and Mourning Doves, Black-chinned Hummingbirds, Bell's Vireos, Yellow-breasted Chats, Summer Tanagers, Painted Buntings, Northern Cardinals, Blue Grosbeaks, and Brown-headed Cowbirds. Other birds that are regular nesters within the floodplain habitat are Yellow-billed Cuckoos, Greater Roadrunners, Screech-Owls, Elf Owls, Ladder-backed Woodpeckers, Black Phoebes, Ash-throated Flycatchers, Verdins, Northern Mockingbirds,

Black-tailed Gnatcatchers, Orchard and Hooded Orioles, Pyrrhuloxias, and House Finches.

In addition to the Rio Grande Village Nature Trail, typical floodplain areas include Hot Springs and the Santa Elena Canyon picnic area. If sufficient water is present to form ponds or marshy areas, as at Rio Grande Village, Pied-billed Grebes, Soras, American Coots, Killdeers, and Common Yellowthroats may find suitable nesting sites.

The *arroyos* offer a drier environment where many of the same birds can often be found nesting. The most conspicuous breeding birds of this community are Verdins, Cactus Wrens, Northern Mockingbirds, Black-tailed Gnatcatchers, Pyrrhuloxias, and House Finches. Scaled Quails and Lesser Nighthawks are ground-nesters that find suitable conditions under the shrubby thickets of mesquite and acacia, and the larger shrubs may offer suitable holes and crevices for nesting Screech-Owls, Elf Owls, Ladder-backed Woodpeckers, and Ash-throated Flycatchers.

Dugout Wells, Glenn Spring, and the Old Sam Nail Ranch—areas that contain permanent water—offer suitable nesting sites for White-winged and Mourning Doves, Yellow-billed Cuckoos, Bell's Vireos, Yellow-breasted Chats, Summer Tanagers, Blue Grosbeaks, Painted Buntings, House Finches, and Lesser Goldfinches.

The *shrub desert* is the largest of Big Bend's plant communities but contains fewer breeding birds than any other habitat. Most important to the nesting birds in this area are the large rocky ledges and cliffs. This habitat is used by Black and Turkey Vultures, Zone-tailed and Red-tailed Hawks, Golden Eagles, American Kestrels, Peregrine and Prairie Falcons, Great Horned Owls, White-throated Swifts, Say's Phoebes, Cliff Swallows, Common Ravens, and Rock and Canyon Wrens. The Cliff Swallow also nests under concrete bridges, such as those over Tornillo Creek.

The plants of the open desert support few breeding birds; the majority of the perching birds seen in this environment nest within adjacent arroyos. Nesting birds of the shrub desert include Scaled Quails, Greater Roadrunners, Ash-throated Flycatchers, Pyrrhuloxias, Black-throated Sparrows, and House Finches. The Black-throated Sparrow is the only species that is more common in this community than in any other.

The *grasslands,* the transition zone between the desert and arroyos and the mountain woodlands, are used by a large number of birds from both of the adjacent communities. Yet in spite of the overlap, there are several species unique to this habitat. Conspicuous grassland birds include Loggerhead Shrikes; Blue Grosbeaks; Varied Buntings; Brown Towhees; Cassin's, Rufous-crowned, and Black-chinned

Sparrows; and Scott's Orioles. Other regular breeding birds of the grasslands include Scaled Quails, Greater Roadrunners, Elf Owls, Common Poorwills, Ladder-backed Woodpeckers, Ash-throated Flycatchers, Verdins, Cactus Wrens, Black-tailed Gnatcatchers, Northern Mockingbirds, Pyrrhuloxias, Black-throated Sparrows, Brown-headed Cowbirds, and House Finches.

Some of the best localities in which to find grassland birds include Government Spring, lower Pine Canyon, Green Gulch, and the central section of the Window Trail. Because of the combined habitats of grasslands and deciduous woodlands along the Window Trail, this can be one of the best places to find a large assortment of birds during summer. A typical list of birds to be seen there is one recorded during the morning of May 25, 1968:

Turkey Vulture
American Kestrel
Scaled Quail
White-winged Dove
Mourning Dove
White-throated Swift
Black-chinned Hummingbird
Blue-throated Hummingbird
Acorn Woodpecker
Say's Phoebe
Ash-throated Flycatcher
Violet-green Swallow
Gray-breasted Jay
Common Raven
Tufted Titmouse
Bushtit
Cactus Wren
Rock Wren
Canyon Wren
Blue-gray Gnatcatcher
Northern Mockingbird
Crissal Thrasher
Gray Vireo
Hepatic Tanager
Summer Tanager
Black-headed Grosbeak
Blue Grosbeak
Varied Bunting
Brown Towhee
Rufous-crowned Sparrow
Brown-headed Cowbird
Scott's Oriole
House Finch
Lesser Goldfinch

The *piñon-juniper-oak woodlands* in the Chisos Mountains may be divided into two different plant associations, deciduous and piñon-juniper. For the most part, these zones of vegetation are interspersed and may be regarded as a single unit. Although a nesting bird may prefer a broadleaf tree over a conifer, it is likely that its total territory includes both. Laguna Meadow is an excellent place to find typical breeding birds of this woodland community, which include Eastern and Western Screech-Owls, Broad-tailed Hummingbirds, Acorn Woodpeckers, Ash-throated Flycatchers, Gray-breasted Jays, Tufted Titmice, Bushtits, Canyon and Bewick's Wrens, Blue-gray Gnatcatchers, Hepatic Tanagers, Black-headed Grosbeaks, Rufous-sided and Brown Towhees, and Rufous-crowned Sparrows. Several species nest within the lower parts of this community and rarely, if ever, breed above

5,000 feet in elevation: White-winged and Mourning Doves, Great Horned and Elf Owls, Black-chinned Hummingbirds, Ladder-backed Woodpeckers, Gray Vireos, Summer Tanagers, Scott's Orioles, Brown-headed Cowbirds, and House Finches. Species that rarely occur in the lower parts of the piñon-juniper-oak woodlands but are fairly common nesters in the highlands include the Zone-tailed Hawk, the Whip-poor-will, the White-breasted Nuthatch, and the Hutton's Vireo.

The *cypress-pine-oak woodlands* are restricted to only a few localities within the Chisos Mountains. Boot Canyon contains the best example of this community, but Pine Canyon offers all of the same birds in summer, with the exception of the Colima Warbler. The most conspicuous breeding birds to be found in Boot Canyon are the Band-tailed Pigeon, Blue-throated and Broad-tailed Hummingbirds, Acorn Woodpecker, Northern Flicker, Western Flycatcher, Gray-breasted Jay, Tufted Titmouse, Canyon Wren, Hutton's Vireo, Colima Warbler, Black-headed Grosbeak, and Rufous-sided Towhee. Less conspicuous but regular nesting birds of this woodland community are the Sharp-shinned Hawk, Flammulated Owl, Whip-poor-will, Bushtit, White-breasted Nuthatch, Bewick's Wren, and Rufous-crowned Sparrow.

The Winter Months

It is reasonably safe to consider the period from mid-November to late February as wintertime in the Big Bend Country. During autumns that are warmer than normal, however, some southward movement may be detected until mid-December. Conversely, colder-than-normal falls may send the majority of migrants south of the border before early November.

Wintering bird populations vary considerably from wet years to dry ones. Sparrows are common following summer and fall periods of above-average precipitation but are usually rare after dry ones. A few groups of birds and individual species are sporadic in occurrence. Waterfowl, hawks, and a number of northern species, such as the Williamson's Sapsucker, Red-breasted Nuthatch, Pygmy Nuthatch, Brown Creeper, Cassin's Finch, and Red Crossbill, may be present during some winters and completely absent in others. During warmer winters, Dusky and Ash-throated Flycatchers, Bewick's Wrens, and Blue-gray Gnatcatchers are more numerous than in colder winters.

The best possible long-term indices to wintering birds are the Christmas Bird Counts. These counts are part of a national bird census, sponsored by the National Audubon Society and the U.S. Fish and Wildlife Service, taken on one day during the last two weeks of each year. The counts indicate bird movement, increases and decreases in populations, and locations of wintering populations. Three different counts were taken each year in Big Bend National Park from 1966 through 1971, in the Rio Grande Village area, the Chisos Mountains, and the Santa Elena Canyon area. Since 1971, at least one count has been taken within the park every year except 1973 and 1974.

The Annotated List of Species

The following is an annotated list of 425 species of birds that have been reported for Big Bend National Park and vicinity. The majority of these—373—are included in the regular list of species, but 52 are regarded as hypothetical and are included in a second list, "Birds of Uncertain Occurrence," which starts on page 257. Common and scientific names used are those given in the American Ornithologists' Union *Check-list of North American Birds,* sixth edition (1983), hereafter referred to as the AOU *Check-list*. I have attempted to identify the observer in giving details of specific sightings; in some cases, however, full names are not known. Any unattributed sightings dated 1966 to 1972 may be assumed to be mine.

Several terms used to describe the status of the various birds within the area are defined as follows:

abundant: Can be found in numbers, without any particular search, in the proper habitat at the right time of year.

common: Can almost always be found, in smaller numbers with a minimum of searching, in the proper habitat at the right time of year.

fairly common: Can sometimes be found, in small numbers and with some searching, in the proper habitat at the right time of year.

uncommon: Is seldom seen, and usually in small numbers or alone, in the proper habitat at the right time of year.

rare: Is encountered only by chance; is found out of its normal range and always comes as a surprise.

A few other terms also need to be clarified:

permanent resident: A bird that remains in the area throughout the year and does not migrate.

summer resident: A bird that breeds in the area; it may arrive as early as March and remain as late as October.

postnesting visitor: A bird that visits the area in summer but does not breed there; one that wanders to the Big Bend after nesting.

migrant: A bird that passes through the area only in spring and/or fall, from March to May and August to November.

winter resident: A bird that remains in the area during winter, arriving as early as September and remaining as late as April.

Loons:
Family Gaviidae

Common Loon

Gavia immer

One record for the park.

The only record for the park is a bird collected on the river near Solis by A. G. Clark on October 17, 1937 (Borell, 1938). Since this species prefers larger bodies of water than those found within the park, it is a vagrant only. Common Loons, however, as well as Arctic (*Gavia arctica*) and Red-throated (*Gavia stellata*) Loons, have been seen on Lake Balmorhea (35 miles north of the Davis Mountains) during the winter months in recent years. The latest spring sighting for Lake Balmorhea is May 14, 1978, by David and Mimi Wolf.

Grebes:
Family Podicipedidae

Least Grebe

Tachybaptus dominicus

Accidental to the Big Bend area, but seems to remain for some time when it occurs.

An individual arrived August 5, 1969, and remained until July 1970. It was seen by numerous birders and photographed by Ty Hotchkiss. On April 15, 1971, I found a lone bird on the Rio Grande silt pond, where the first bird had last been seen. And it was again recorded at Rio Grande Village from December 12, 1978, through April 1, 1979 (Rick LoBello).

Pied-billed Grebe

Podilymbus podiceps

Rare summer and winter resident; fairly common migrant.

The scarcity of water areas throughout the Big Bend limits the Pied-billed Grebe as a nesting species. Even at suitable habitats, such as the cattail-filled silt pond at Rio Grande Village, it does not nest every year. Roger Siglin observed an adult with young on its back there on July 28, 1967, and I found four free-swimming, fledged young on August 1. On May 17, 1970, I again heard and observed two birds courting at the same pond. They remained there throughout the summer and presumably nested. It is of interest that the birds nested there only in 1967 and 1970, the only two years that the silt pond was dredged. Perhaps their nesting requirements exclude a pond without an adjacent deep pond or running channel.

Pied-billed Grebes are most often seen on open, quiet stretches of river and on adjacent ponds during migration from early March through May and September 1 to November 23.

Eared Grebe

Podiceps nigricollis

Uncommon fall migrant; rare spring migrant; uncommon in winter on the Rio Grande and adjacent ponds.

The majority of sightings have been reported from Rio Grande Village and vicinity from October 26 through mid-March. A May 14, 1978, sighting by Texas Ornithological Society members at Lake Balmorhea is the latest record for the region.

Pelicans: *Family Pelecanidae*

American White Pelican

Pelecanus erythrorhynchos

Four records for the Big Bend Country.

Louise and Henry Hoffman first reported it from near Santa Elena Canyon, May 18 through 24, 1957. On April 1, 1963, park ranger Lloyd Whitt acquired a bird band taken from a "large white bird" found dead in the Rio Grande near Castolon by a Mexican boy who had carried the band in his pocket for more than a year. U.S. Fish and Wildlife Service records showed it to be from a White Pelican banded at Gunnison Island on the Great Salt Lake in Utah, June 19, 1947. Rich Simmons and Jay Liggett observed a lone bird in the river below Boquillas Canyon Overlook on June 16, 1983. J. A. Roosevelt found a White Pelican at Roosevelt Lake, in western Jeff Davis County, in April 1956.

Cormorants: *Family Phalacrocoracidae*

Olivaceous Cormorant

Phalacrocorax olivaceus

Two reports for the Big Bend Country.

Thompson G. Marsh observed two along Terlingua Creek, at the mouth of Santa Elena Canyon, on March 23, 1960, and described them as being the size of mergansers. Twenty-two days later, on April 14, Harold Brodrick found a lone bird on the river at Solis, more than forty miles below Santa Elena Canyon.

Herons, Bitterns: *Family Ardeidae*

American Bittern

Botaurus lentiginosus

Uncommon migrant (April 17–May 20, September 30–November 10).

There are also two winter and one early spring sightings: Peter Lesica reported one at Rio Grande Village on December 10, 1978; Bonnie McKinney found one at a lake on the Sombrero Peak Ranch (just north of the park) on February 15, 1983; and I recorded one at Rio Grande Village on March 24, 1970.

Least Bittern

Ixobrychus exilis

Rare summer resident and migrant.

There are no park records before 1966. A pair of Least Bitterns resided at the Rio Grande

Village silt pond during June 1967, and I observed another pair there on May 11, 1969, but I did not find a nest or see young birds either year. Other sightings, all at Rio Grande Village, include lone birds seen on April 20, 1967, and April 15, 1971 (Wauer), April 27, 1966 (David and Roy Brown), May 6, 1970 (Doyle and Helen Peckham and Wauer), September 9, 1967 (Wauer), October 27, 1977 (J. H. and E. G. Strauss), and November 23, 1977 (John Duncan). This extremely shy bird may be more common in migration than records indicate.

Great Blue Heron

Ardea herodias

Rare in summer; fairly common migrant and winter visitor.

This large, graceful bird appears to be present along the Rio Grande all year. There are no records of nesting, although Sutton (1935) did observe an adult and an immature bird near Boquillas, Coahuila, on May 21, 1935. It is likely that this species once nested along the river, but today, between Boquillas and Presidio, there is only one grove of cottonwoods and willows large enough to support a rookery; it is located on the floodplain near Santa Elena Crossing, where there is probably too much human activity for nesting herons.

Sightings increase during late September, and migrants are most common from mid-October to early November and from early March through the first week of May. Wintering birds can be expected anywhere along the river and at adjacent ponds.

Great Egret

Casmerodius albus

Uncommon migrant and occasional throughout the summer.

Records range from April 8 through October 12. Most sightings are of lone birds, but 82 were recorded at the north end of Black Gap Wildlife Management Area, on October 5, 1982, by Bonnie McKinney.

Snowy Egret

Egretta thula

Uncommon spring migrant (April 11–May 13); two fall sightings.

Vaughn Morrison saw it at Rio Grande Village on September 13, 1974, and I recorded it on September 14, 1969. One later record is of "several on trees and on rooftops" at Panther Junction on November 4, 1975 (Frank Deckert).

Little Blue Heron

Egretta caerulea

Six records for the park.

Records range from March 11 through October 12, and all are of lone birds, except for a sighting of four individuals near Alamo Creek by Paul Strong, July 28, 1980.

Tricolored Heron

Egretta tricolor

Rare migrant and regular postnesting visitor along the river and at adjacent ponds.

Although there were no records of this beautiful bird before 1967, since then it has been seen on several occasions from April 5 to May 24 and August 1 to September 11. I have found it surprisingly unafraid at times; more than once I have walked to within a few yards of birds feeding along the shore of the larger pond at Rio Grande Village.

Cattle Egret

Bubulcus ibis

Common migrant (March 29–May 29, August 26–November 8).

This species has increased dramatically within the Big Bend Country in recent years, and it can be expected throughout the winter months at grassy areas along the Rio Grande. It was first reported at Rio Grande Village, by Roger Siglin and Gary Blyth, on October 27, 1967. Most sightings come from along the Rio Grande and along the Tornillo Creek drainage. Although there are no records above the Panther Junction area, its presence in the Basin may be anticipated.

Green-backed Heron

Butorides striatus

Uncommon in summer and winter; fairly common in migration.

The spring migration is heavier than the fall, and the northern movement reaches a peak between May 1 and 19. Postnesting wanderers and early fall migrants may appear by mid-August. The fall migration seems to start early and drag along to mid-November, with a two-week peak in early September. An occasional bird will remain at suitable locations, such as Rio Grande Village, throughout mild winters. Most records are from the lowlands, but Pansy Espy reported this heron at 6,000 feet at a stock tank near Pine Peak in the Davis Mountains on October 10, 1969.

Although there are no recent records of nesting, the Green-backed Heron is present along the river during May and June, and nesting is likely at appropriate places along the floodplain. Van Tyne and Sutton (1937) discovered a nest, containing four eggs, twelve feet up in a mesquite near the river at Castolon on May 7, 1935. The breeding race was identified as the western form, *anthonyi*. Palmer (1962) reported that the eastern race is known to nest eastward from Pecos and Fort Stockton, Texas.

Black-crowned Night-Heron

Nycticorax nycticorax

Rare migrant that can occur at any time of the year along the Rio Grande and at adjacent ponds.

Van Tyne and Sutton (1937) reported it to be fairly common along the river in May, but there were only three park sightings during the 1960s, only one in the 1970s, and five from 1980 through 1983. Paul Strong reported an immature bird at Rio Grande Village on August 25, 1980.

Yellow-crowned Night-Heron

Nycticorax violaceus

Rare migrant and regular postnesting visitor along the river and adjacent ponds.

It is strange that there were no reports of this nocturnal heron in the Big Bend area before 1967. I have found it a visitor to be expected at the ponds at Rio Grande Village after July 23. Fall migrants have been recorded as late as October 12; I took a specimen there on September 13, 1967. The majority of these late summer and fall birds are juveniles. There is but one series of spring sightings—a lone bird at Rio Grande Village from April 26 to May 6, 1968 (Wauer and Paul and Martha Whitson).

Ibises, Spoonbills: *Family Threskiornithidae*

White Ibis

Eudocimus albus

Only one record for the park.

Mr. and Mrs. Joe Maxwell observed and photographed one along irrigation ditches at Rio Grande Village on February 6 or 7, 1971. It apparently was killed by a predator, because Philip F. Allan reported a dead White Ibis on February 8. The specimen was examined by Art Norton, who retained a number of feathers. I later obtained several characteristic primaries and deposited them in the Big Bend National Park study collection.

White-faced Ibis

Plegadis chihi

Rare migrant (March 31–May 29, August 11–September 25).

There is also a single winter record of twenty birds seen at Boquillas, Coahuila, during a dust storm, on January 25, 1965.

Storks: *Family Ciconiidae*

Wood Stork

Mycteria americana

Two records for the park.

Jerry Strickling first observed one perched on a cottonwood tree at Dugout Wells on May 18, 1962; and Kristin Larson reported an immature bird along the Rio Grande in Boquillas Canyon on May 12, 1983.

Swans, Geese, Ducks: *Family Anatidae*

Fulvous Whistling-Duck

Dendrocygna bicolor

One sighting for the park.

A lone bird was observed sitting on the Mexican bank of the river across from Rio Grande Village, April 18, 1967, by five capable birders whom I recorded only as Hanlon, McCarroll, Meyer, Kuehn, and Rowe. Pansy Espy recorded one at the Caldwell Ranch in the Davis Mountains in September 1965.

Tundra Swan

Cygnus columbianus

Four records for the Big Bend Country.

William Lay Thompson (1953) reported twelve individuals at a stock tank at Black Gap Wildlife Management Area, just north of the park, in December 1951; all twelve were reportedly killed by local ranchers. Clay Miller found seven of these birds near Valentine on December 12, 1961. Dick Youse observed three birds on the river at Rio Grande Village on December 30, 1969, and Dennis Prichard reported one from there December 9, 1979.

Greater White-fronted Goose

Anser albifrons

Three records for the park.

Ty and Julie Hotchkiss saw it first along the river at Rio Grande Village on April 29, 1969, and reported it to me the following day. After trying unsuccessfully to find the bird on May 1,

I asked some of the Mexican boys at Boquillas Crossing if any of them had seen a *pato grande* (large duck). Siverio Athayde said that he had seen a large waterbird the previous day. Without hesitation, he picked the White-fronted Goose out of a three-page series of pictures of ducks and geese in *Birds of North America*.

More recently, on March 31, 1983, a lone female was observed at Rio Grande Village by C. Lippincott; and on April 10, 1983, two individuals were reported on the Rio Grande five to ten miles south of Talley by H. P. Langridge and George Wagner.

Snow Goose

Chen caerulescens

Rare winter visitor (November 1–March 31).

Most records are of lone birds along the Rio Grande. However, Rick LoBello observed fifteen birds over Rio Grande Village in February, and Curt Fitrow reported thirteen on March 18, 1979. A dead bird was found on the highway four miles northwest of Alpine by Joe Marshall on March 31, 1977, and was placed in the Sul Ross State University collection.

Ross' Goose

Chen rossii

One record from Jeff Davis County.

Joe Robinette collected one from a stock tank on the Wittenburg Ranch on January 30, 1970. It is now in the Sul Ross State University collection.

A FIELD GUIDE TO BIRDS OF THE BIG BEND

Turkey Vulture	Rock Wren
American Kestrel	Canyon Wren
Scaled Quail	Blue-gray Gnatcatcher
White-winged Dove	Northern Mockingbird
Mourning Dove	Crissal Thrasher
White-throated Swift	Gray Vireo
Black-chinned Hummingbird	Hepatic Tanager
Blue-throated Hummingbird	Summer Tanager
Acorn Woodpecker	Black-headed Grosbeak
Say's Phoebe	Blue Grosbeak
Ash-throated Flycatcher	Varied Bunting
Violet-green Swallow	Brown Towhee
Gray-breasted Jay	Rufous-crowned Sparrow
Common Raven	Brown-headed Cowbird
Tufted Titmouse	Scott's Oriole
Bushtit	House Finch
Cactus Wren	Lesser Goldfinch

Avocets, Stilts: *Family Recurvirostridae*

Black-necked Stilt

Himantopus mexicanus

Rare migrant (March 23–May 24, August 18–October 3).

There is one wintertime report from Rio Grande Village on January 25, 1979, by Robert DeVine. This species is fairly common in spring and fall at Lake Balmorhea.

American Avocet

Recurvirostra americana

Uncommon spring migrant (April 10–June 1); rare in fall and summer.

There is a scattering of reports through the summer: Bill Graber found four at Hot Springs on June 28, 1983; Robert DeVine reported one there on July 28, 1981; David Easterla observed one south of the park at a pond near Las Norias, Coahuila, Mexico, on August 10, 1970; and Cindy Simmons reported four individuals at Rio Grande Village on August 11, 1983. Fall records include fifteen birds seen along the river between Castolon and Santa Elena Canyon on September 24, 1967, and one at Rio Grande Village on October 6, 1970 (Wauer). All of the above sightings are for the lowlands on or near the Rio Grande; an exception to this is a sighting of a lone bird at the Chisos Basin sewage lagoons, by Anne Bellamy, on April 12, 1982.

The breeding range of this wader extends as far south as southern New Mexico and San Luis Potosí, Mexico (AOU, 1983), and east from near Midland, Texas, to the central and southern Gulf Coast (Oberholser, 1974). Nesting within the Big Bend at suitable ponds is possible.

Sandpipers, Snipes, Woodcocks, Phalaropes: *Family Scolopacidae*

Greater Yellowlegs

Tringa melanoleuca

Fairly common migrant (March 17–April 13, July 14–October 15) along the Rio Grande and adjacent ponds.

There is a late spring sighting at Rio Grande Village on May 20, 1968 (Wauer).

Lesser Yellowlegs

Tringa flavipes

Uncommon migrant (April 1–May 11, July 17–October 26).

Lone birds may be expected at old stock ponds on the desert as well as along the river, and five were seen at a flooded field at Rio Grande Village on September 16, 1970 (Wauer). There is also one winter sighting: Peter and Ruth Isleib found it at Rio Grande Village February 3 to 5, 1965.

Solitary Sandpiper

Tringa solitaria

Fairly common migrant (March 23–May 10, July 15–October 12); somewhat sporadic in occurrence.

Migrants are not restricted to the river but can be expected anywhere below 4,000 feet; there are several sightings from Maverick and Panther Junction. Most records are of lone birds, but I saw a flock of seven at Rio Grande Village on August 5, 1969.

Willet

Catoptrophorus semipalmatus

Rare migrant (March 10–May 20); only two fall sightings.

I found sixteen birds bathing along the river at Rio Grande Village on August 15, 1969, and John MacDonald and Tom Myer reported one there on August 19, 1970. This is a common migrant at Lake Balmorhea.

Spotted Sandpiper

Actitis macularia

Common migrant and winter resident along the river and at adjacent ponds.

Except for a brief period from June 13 to July 16, it has been found throughout the year. Fall migrants reach a peak from mid-August until the last of September, and northbound birds are most numerous from mid-March through May 21. Migrants occur at stock ponds throughout the desert, and I saw one in the Chisos Basin at the sewage lagoons on September 15, 1968. In winter Spotted Sandpipers can be seen almost anywhere along the river; I found more than thirty while rafting through Mariscal Canyon on February 1, 1968.

Upland Sandpiper

Bartramia longicauda

Rare spring and uncommon fall migrant.

Spring records range from April 3 (Bert Schaughency) to May 11 (Wauer), and fall records from July 31 (Scott Lanier) to September 12 (near Marathon by David Wolf, 1973). All of these sightings are of one, two, or three birds, but David Easterla and Jim Tucker recorded twelve individuals at an irrigated field at Rio Grande Village on August 30, 1970.

Judge Charley Shannon says that these birds were once fairly common migrants around Marfa, but he rarely hears them pass overhead now.

Whimbrel

Numenius phaeopus

Only two records for the Big Bend.

Harold Brodrick reported one near Panther Junction on April 27, 1957, and Robert M. LaVal saw one along Tornillo Creek at Hot Springs on April 26, 1969. He reported it to me, and I found it still there two days later. It was collected and represents the first specimen of this species for West Texas.

Long-billed Curlew

Numenius americanus

Uncommon migrant (March 16–May 21, August 16–September 12).

It was first observed by Lovie Mae Whitaker at Hot Springs in September 1935. Doug Evans and Bruce Shaw observed and photographed one on Tornillo Flat on May 27, 1964. Most sightings have been of two or three birds, but Dick Strange saw a flock of eight at Rio Grande Village on April 14, 1965, and I found seven there on April 11, 1967. This long-legged shorebird prefers open, grassy areas and is seldom seen along the river.

Western Sandpiper

Calidris mauri

Rare migrant and winter visitor.

There is only one spring sighting: Van Tyne and Sutton (1937) saw three birds feeding along the river at Lajitas on May 10, 1935. I have found fall migrants at Rio Grande Village on three occasions: two on September 3 and four on September 10, 1966, and two on September 6, 1967. Two winter records exist, at Rio Grande Village on December 8 and 27 (Wauer).

Least Sandpiper

Calidris minutilla

Fairly common migrant and uncommon winter visitor along the river and at adjacent water areas.

This is the most numerous of Big Bend's "peeps." It has been recorded every month but May and June. Spring sightings range from mid-March to April 30; I found twelve birds, a high count, near Boquillas Crossing on April 5, 1970. Fall migrants reach the Big Bend as early as July 14, and this bird can be expected at suitable places throughout the fall and winter. I have seen it regularly in winter along lower Tornillo Creek, at Hot Springs, and along Calamity Creek just south of Alpine on Highway 118.

Long-billed Dowitcher

Limnodromus scolopaceus

Six sightings in the park area.

Only two of the six sightings were positively of Long-bills: Dave Snyder heard and observed one from only a few yards away at Cottonwood Campground on August 27, 1971, and Vicki Glen heard and observed two at Rio Grande Village on October 9, 1982. These are the only fall records. There are two spring records—April 15, 1971 (O. J. Theobald), and May 2, 1969 (Wauer)—and three winter records: one at Hot Springs on December 30, 1967 (Barbara Ribble and Ruth Black); one at Rio Grande Village on December 30, 1969 (Wauer); and one at Black Gap Wildlife Management Area, just north of the park, on February 4, 1982 (Bonnie

McKinney). This species apparently is a common migrant in the vicinity of Lake Balmorhea; Jim Scudday collected four individuals there on April 6, 1967.

Common Snipe

Gallinago gallinago

Uncommon migrant and winter visitor.

Records of this snipe range from August 31 through May 11, but it is most numerous as a fall migrant from October 15 to November 5. A few can usually be found at pond edges and irrigation ditches at Rio Grande Village and Cottonwood Campground all winter. There is a slight increase in numbers toward the end of March as spring migrants pass through the area. This northbound movement, which is not as great at that in the fall, subsides by mid-April, but stragglers continue to be seen until May 11. Most records are of lone birds, but I found twelve together at Rio Grande Village on September 29, 1970.

American Woodcock

Scolopax minor

Four sightings (October 6–November 24).

All records are from Rio Grande Village.

Wilson's Phalarope

Phalaropus tricolor

Uncommon spring migrant (April 15–May 6); rare fall migrant (August 11–September 20).

The largest number reported was thirteen at the Rio Grande Village sewage lagoon on August 11, 1983, by Cindy Simmons. There is also a record of the Red-necked Phalarope (*Phalaropus lobatus*) for the Big Bend area: Jim Scudday collected one at Lake Balmorhea on October 21, 1969.

Gulls, Terns:
Family Laridae

Laughing Gull

Larus atricilla

Three records for the Big Bend Country.

The first record is of a dead bird found at an earthen tank at Black Gap Wildlife Management Area in June 1951 (Thompson, 1953). David Easterla observed an adult near Terlingua Creek at Terlingua Abaja on June 4, 1973, and Paul Strong and B. Alex reported one at Panther Junction on October 19, 1983.

Franklin's Gull

Larus pipixcan

Rare migrant (April 14–June 10, October 19–November 13).

Two of the records are rather interesting. On the very windy morning of April 14, 1971, I observed 29 black-and-white gulls flying together up Tornillo Creek, near the lower bridge, at about 7:00. At 10:30 the same morning, Dick Brownstein, Ed Seeker, Paul Benham, and Joe Grzybowski saw 29 Franklin's Gulls flying north about 20 miles south of Marathon. If both sightings were of the same 29 gulls, they traveled 55 miles in three and a half hours.

On October 19, 1983, Bonnie McKinney observed and photographed nine immature gulls at Black Gap Wildlife Management Area headquarters. The photographs were later sent to Dr. Keith Arnold of Texas A&M University, who identified the birds as being of this species.

Ring-billed Gull

Larus delawarensis

Five park records.

Felix Hernandez III and I saw four individuals (three adults and one immature) resting on a sandbar near Boquillas Crossing on April 26, 1968; Susan and Richard Block reported one at Hot Springs on March 8, 1969; Mark Hoffman found one at Rio Grande Village on July 5, 1977; A. Weaks found one at Boquillas on October 12, 1983; and J. Pace reported one at Rio Grande Village on November 19, 1983. This species has been reported regularly at Lake Balmorhea in fall, winter, and spring.

Forster's Tern

Sterna forsteri

Four park records.

This species was first reported by Charles Gill for Rio Grande Village on May 1, 1976. One bird at Rio Grande Village was reported by Ken Soltesz on May 9, 1978, and by Mimi Wolf the following day. And Bonnie McKinney found one at Black Gap Wildlife Management Area on March 20, 1982.

Least Tern

Sterna antillarum

Two records for the park.

Maxilla Evans observed a lone bird flying over the Rio Grande at Talley, just west of Mariscal Canyon, on April 4, 1969; and Helene Watson reported one at Rio Grande Village on May 8, 1978. It appears to be more common north of the park in the Davis Mountains and Balmorhea area; Pansy Espy recorded it there in February, June, and September.

Pigeons, Doves: *Family Columbidae*

Rock Dove

Columba livia

A rare visitor to the park.

This is the domestic pigeon of American cities. All park sightings date from June 10 through August 16, and most were made at Rio Grande Village or Panther Junction. The most interesting of these sightings occurred on June 24, 1970, at Rio Grande Village, when David Easterla watched a Peregrine Falcon capture one of two Rock Doves.

Band-tailed Pigeon

Columba fasciata

Fairly common summer resident and sporadic winter resident in the Chisos Mountains.

The Band-tailed Pigeon may first be detected by its owllike *oo-whoo* call, which can be rather ventriloquistic within the narrow canyons. It can usually be found in Boot and Pine canyons throughout the year, but it visits lower canyons during periods of good acorn crops. Seventy birds, a high count, were found in Boot Canyon on August 8, 1969 (Wauer). In July and August of 1969 and 1970 this species could be found in numbers in the oak groves along the Window Trail. Walter Rooney, who lived at Oak Creek (just below the Window) from 1916 to 1923, told Doug Evans that "millions of pigeons" came into Oak Creek, scattered over a mile "like the wind blowing," when the acorns were on the trees (Rooney, 1966). One pigeon that was killed had 28 acorns in it.

Apparently, an occasional bird may move out of the mountains altogether in the fall; Charles Bender saw one at Dugout Wells on August 21, 1966. On May 11, 1968, I found five birds feeding among the oaks at an elevation of 4,800 feet in lower Green Gulch.

Band-tailed Pigeon, *Columba fasciata*

Nesting occurs from April through September. There are two recent records: Pete Peterson found a nest containing two eggs near the Boot Spring cabin on July 24, 1981; and Brete Griffin reported a nest 25 feet high in a ponderosa pine on the upper north slope of Pine Canyon on August 6, 1982.

In winter this species appears to be common at times but very difficult to find at others.

On December 23, 1968, Christmas bird counters Roger Siglin and Dick Nelson tallied 58 individuals in Boot Canyon. I found it common there on January 27 and February 22, 1968, and again on March 9, 1969, but I did not find a single one there on January 28 and 29, 1967. It is also sporadic in winter in the Davis Mountains, according to wildlife conservation officer Harvey Adams. I have seen it near the roadway in Madera Canyon in November, December, and January.

White-winged Dove

Zenaida asiatica

Fairly common permanent resident.

The majority, if not all, of the park's White-wings are resident; one banded at Panther Junction on April 23, 1968, was recaptured there on February 3 and June 6, 1969. They are found at mesquite thickets along the river, in adjacent washes, at springs below 5,000 feet, and locally within the lower canyons of the Chisos Mountains.

Lowland birds begin to pair early in February, and the earliest *who-cooks-for-whoo* call was heard on February 14. I found one nest on a branch of an Emory oak along the Window Trail on May 11, 1968, and another 45 feet above the ground on the branch of a huge cottonwood at Boquillas on May 21, 1968. I frightened two juveniles from a nest in lower Blue Creek Canyon on June 8, 1971. Nesting continues into July; I found a pair building a nest at Rio Grande Village on July 18, 1970. White-wings are most difficult to find during the latter part of the nesting period.

In winter the birds flock at preferred areas, such as Rio Grande Village (I found 70 there on January 22, 1970), Dugout Wells, Panther Junction (I found 22 birds there on November 10, 1967), and along the Window Trail. The park's White-wings are considered to be of the "Mexican Highland" race of central Mexico and the

White-winged Dove, *Zenaida asiatica*

lower Big Bend Country, according to Cottam and Trefethen's very thorough analysis (1968).

Mourning Dove

Zenaida macroura

Common summer resident and migrant; fairly common winter resident along the river floodplain, at springs, and in washes and canyons below 5,000 feet.

Some birds are permanent residents. Birds banded at Panther Junction include one banded on April 6, 1967, and recaptured on April 13 and December 8, 1969; another banded on January 22, 1968, was recaptured on May 25, 1968, and January 30, 1969; and one banded on March 26, 1968, was recaptured on December 2, 1968.

Nesting occurs from March through June most years, much later during wet years. During the fall of 1966, I found a nest with one egg on a cottonwood at Rio Grande Village as late as September 17. And Felix Hernandez III reported finding a nest on the ground under a creosote bush at Castolon on July 8, 1981. Wintering birds are usually found in small flocks of ten to twenty.

Inca Dove

Columbina inca

Uncommon summer resident and migrant (March 27–May 20, August 6–early November); rare in winter.

It appears that this little dove has decreased in numbers since pre-park days. Van Tyne and Sutton (1937) found it "almost daily at Castolon . . . inhabiting the mesquite bordering and cultivated fields." It favors areas of human habitation and breeds at Mexican dwellings and villages across the river; Smith (1936) reported it feeding with chickens at Boquillas during June and July 1936. There are two records of breeding within the park: I found a copulating pair at Rio Grande Village on May 7, 1971; and Darryl Rathban observed two at a nest on a cottonwood tree at Rio Grande Village on August 3, 1982.

Common Ground-Dove

Columbina passerina

Uncommon summer resident and migrant; sporadic in winter at a few localities.

The Common Ground-Dove nests in mesquite thickets along the river and in adjacent flats, such as those at Rio Grande Village, where it was found nest-building on June 23,

1969, and incubating two eggs on September 7, 1968 (Wauer). It is most common in migration from March 20 through May and from mid-August through October. Sightings away from the vicinity of the Rio Grande are few: a lone bird was seen at Panther Junction on April 6, 1967, and one was banded there on September 1, 1969. In winter it is usually present in small numbers on open weedy and mesquite flats along the river (I found seven near Castolon on January 25, 1969), but apparently it is sporadic in occurrence. I could not find a single bird during the cool, dry winter of 1969–70.

White-tipped Dove

Leptotila verreauxi

Only three park sightings.

The species was first reported from Dugout Wells and the Chisos Basin by Alexander Sprunt, Jr., June 10 and 12, 1956. I found a lone bird at Rio Grande Village on June 30, 1970.

Cuckoos, Roadrunners, Anis: *Family Cuculidae*

Yellow-billed Cuckoo

Coccyzus americanus

Fairly common summer resident.

This cuckoo is commonly found at cottonwood groves along the Rio Grande, such as those at Rio Grande Village and Cottonwood Campground, and less commonly at riparian areas up to 5,500 feet. On June 30, 1971, I heard one calling in lower Boot Canyon. This is one of the last summer residents to arrive on its breeding grounds. H. T. Hargis recorded it as early as April 27; it may stay as late as September 24 but becomes quite scarce by August 20. Nesting records (all at Rio Grande Village) include two nests found on cottonwoods on June 8, 1969, and another containing one egg discovered on a mesquite on July 23, 1968; I saw an adult feeding a cicada to a nestling on July 31. On September 8, 1969, I observed a roadrunner with a recently captured young Yellow-billed Cuckoo.

Greater Roadrunner

Geococcyx californianus

Fairly common resident in the lowlands and less so up to 5,500 feet.

I know of no better place to find this ground cuckoo than at Rio Grande Village, where it is numerous. Courting begins in February; I heard the first "bark" of the season at Rio Grande Village on February 15, 1968, and nest-building was taking place in mid-March. I found one egg laid in a nest there on March 20. Other nesting records include one nest with three eggs there on March 31, 1970 (Murl Deusing), one with three eggs near the Chisos Basin sewage lagoons on May 25, 1969, one with three eggs

Greater Roadrunner, *Geococcyx californianus*

and three young at Rio Grande Village on June 19, 1968, and another there with two young ready to leave the nest on August 5, 1969. Bruce Stewart reported observing a roadrunner beating a Ladder-backed Woodpecker to death at Rio Grande Village on December 25, 1977.

Groove-billed Ani

Crotophaga sulcirostris

Regular late spring and summer visitor (April 20–October 19).

This species appears to be increasing in West Texas. The first record for the Trans-Pecos was one collected north of the park at Black Gap by W. F. Blair in June 1951 (Thompson, 1953). Roger Siglin saw one at Rio Grande Village and watched it for several minutes before it flew across the river on August 4, 1967. On May 21, 1968, one of two birds seen at Rio Grande Village was collected (Wauer, 1968*b*).

Since these first records, the Groove-billed Ani has become a regular late spring and summer visitor at Rio Grande Village and adjacent floodplain, arriving in June and remaining until October; the most recent sighting is one by Gene Blacklock and Bruce Fall at Rio Grande Village on October 19, 1974. Although there are no records of a successful nesting, a pair built a nest along the Rio Grande Village Nature Trail on July 26, 1969; they deserted this nest within a few days but constructed two more in a cottonwood at the pond next to the campground, August 5 and 12. These nests were deserted as well. An additional sighting is one at the Miller Ranch by the Millers and Pansy Espy on November 10, 1969.

Barn Owls:
Family Tytonidae

Common Barn-Owl

Tyto alba

Rare migrant.

There are scattered records for the park from April 20 to May 24 in spring; there is a lone summertime report of one at Rio Grande Village on July 24, 1980, by Bruce Hallett; and there are two fall reports: David Wolf found a feather at Rio Grande Village on September 7, 1973, and C. Philip Allen observed one at Devil's Den on September 9, 1963. Bonnie McKinney found a road-kill one mile west of Marathon on November 9, 1983.

Typical Owls:
Family Strigidae

Flammulated Owl

Otus flammeolus

Fairly common summer resident (March 30–September 24) at localized highland areas.

The Flammulated Owl has been found most often in Boot Canyon, where I saw a juvenile with a captured monarch butterfly on June 8, 1968. During April and May it can usually be called up right after dark with a few hoots that need only partially resemble the deep *boot* call of this bird. One must stay overnight at Boot Spring, however, to be assured of seeing it. It begins its nightly activities about one hour after sunset—approximately 10:00 to 10:15 p.m. in May and June—and is usually found in the main canyon just below the cabin. It also has been seen on the north slope of Casa Grande on two occasions: N. C. Hazard photographed one there on April 19, 1965, and Dave and Ginger Harwood saw two birds there on April 20, 1970.

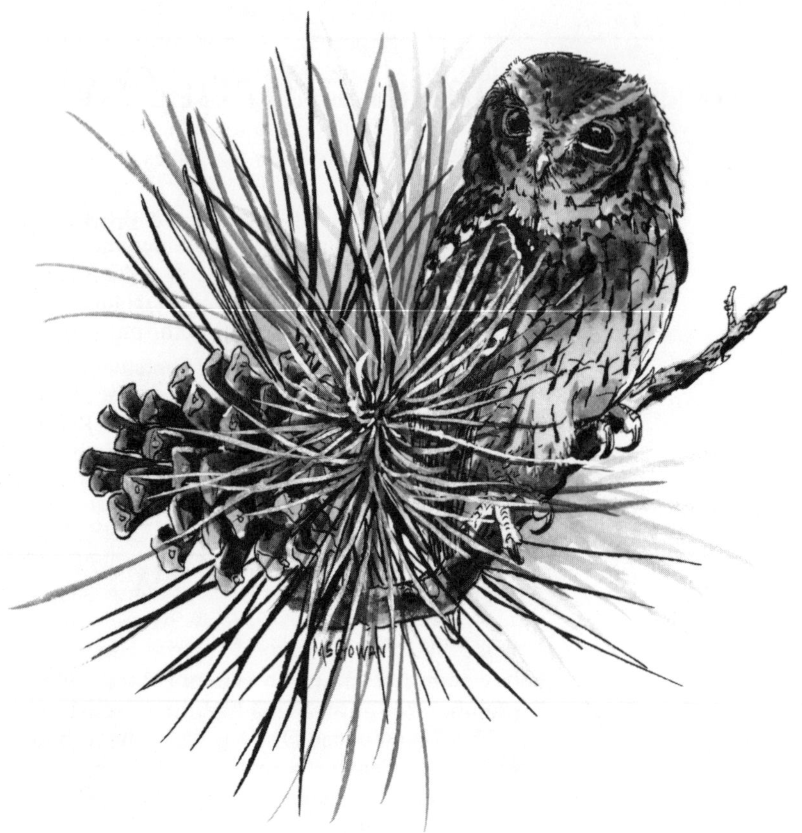

Flammulated Owl, *Otus flammeolus*

Eastern Screech-Owl

Otus asio

Western Screech-Owl

Otus kennicottii

Fairly common permanent residents.

The revised AOU *Check-list* (1983) split the former Screech Owl into these two species. Since field observations alone cannot separate the two forms, and all previous records have been kept together, they will be considered together here. This is not to say that some of the new records cannot be kept separate, because the eastern bird has a characteristic quavering whistle, while the western bird gives a "bouncing-ball" call.

Marshall (1967) discovered that the Big Bend represents the only North American area where the two birds overlap. He found a mixed pair with grown young at Boquillas in July 1962. It is not unusual to hear both songs from anywhere in the park.

The Screech Owl utilizes thickets of mesquite and willows along the river and the piñon-juniper-oak woodlands in the mountains. Nesting has been documented from early March through July. Bruce Talbot reported a nest at Rio Grande Village on March 12, 1983; I found an adult carrying food to a hole in a large willow tree at Boquillas on June 8, 1967; a nest was discovered near Nine Point Draw by the park maintenance crew on June 28, 1974; Harold Brodrick observed a pair with three youngsters at the K-Bar Ranch on June 29, 1960; and David Easterla found two adults feeding young at Boot Spring on July 9, 1968.

Great Horned Owl

Bubo virginianus

Fairly common summer and winter resident and migrant below 5,500 feet.

This is the regularly seen large owl of the river canyons, floodplain, and desert springs. It is likely that most of the park's birds are permanent residents, but there is a distinct increase in sightings from March 22 to May 26 and from early September through November 23. This owl is considered one of the park's major predators; George Howarth and Margaret Littlejohn found one with a dead ring-tail cat at Panther Pass on January 19, 1978.

Northern Pygmy-Owl

Glaucidium gnoma

Five park records (August 7–September 28).

It is likely that Big Bend's pygmy-owls are postnesting visitors from the Maderas del Carmens, the forested mountains less than fifty miles southeast of the Chisos Mountains in Mexico (Wauer and Ligon, 1977). The first park records were of lone birds calling at Boot Spring at dawn on August 10 and September 28, 1969 (Wauer). Benton Basham reported one ten to twelve miles north of Panther Junction, in the middle of the road, on September 22, 1977. And there were two records for Boot Spring in August 1982: Kenneth Danney heard one on August 7, and Greg Lasley heard and later observed one there on August 12.

Elf Owl

Micrathene whitneyi

Fairly common summer resident and migrant below 5,600 feet.

Park records range from March 12 through September 18. The Elf Owl apparently migrates along the river, because it is common there first, arriving at Panther Junction in another five to eight days; the earliest Chisos Basin record is April 17. Early birds are very vociferous and call from "posts" along the edges of their territories. By mid- to late April, however, when their territories have been defined and nesting has begun, they become quieter and more difficult to find.

Quillin (1935) found the Elf Owl nesting in Juniper Canyon on May 21, 1934. Two or three pairs use the Rio Grande Village area; specimens can usually can be found at Dugout Wells; and several pairs nest along the Window Trail

Elf Owl, *Micrathene whitneyi*

and near the Basin Amphitheatre. By late June the birds become very quiet but can often be found at night hunting moths around lights at Rio Grande Village and in the Chisos Basin. They also are sometimes seen along the park roads, where they suddenly fly up alongside a passing automobile. I have found family groups in mesquite thickets after nesting as well: three individuals at Dugout Wells on July 4, 1968, and three there on August 17, 1968. The status of this little owl within the southwestern United States was summarized by Barlow and Johnson (1967).

Burrowing Owl

Athene cunicularia

Rare in the park.

There are only sixteen sightings, which range from October 31 through June 27. There is one record of nesting: I found a pair at a burrow near the Loop Camp turnoff of the River Road on April 17, 1969. It is more common in open fields from Fort Davis to Balmorhea and east to Sanderson during spring and early summer.

Long-eared Owl

Asio otus

Rare summer visitor to the mountains; rare migrant and winter visitor.

It may nest at Boot Spring; I heard it calling there on June 11, 1967, and June 7, 1970. There are a handful of records from the lowlands that range from September 16 (one found dead along the road near Study Butte by J. W. Duffield in 1977) through May 10 (a lone bird seen at San Vicente by Van Tyne and Sutton [1937] in 1933). Pansy Espy recorded it in the Davis Mountains only during December, and Jody Miller found a dead bird at the Miller Ranch on April 22, 1961.

Short-eared Owl

Asio flammeus

Five records for the park.

I first found a lone bird at Dugout Wells on April 27, 1968. Charles Crabtree observed five or six individuals at Rice Tank on January 4, 1971, and Bill Mealy reported one just south of Persimmon Gap on March 28, 1978. There are two 1981 records: B. D. Leopold found four in a wash two miles west of Grapevine Hills on February 10, and John Morlock reported two between Pantera and the Johnson Ranch on July 18 and 19.

Jim Scudday collected a specimen eleven miles east of Lake Balmorhea on January 29, 1969, and the Clay Millers recorded the species at their ranch near Valentine in December 1955 and on November 1 and 16, 1959. It may be more common within the northern portion of the Big Bend Country than the few park records indicate.

Northern Saw-whet Owl

Aegolius acadicus

Three records for the park.

I first heard one calling near Boot Spring after dark on November 3, 1967, but I could not call it close enough for a good look. Then, on February 23, 1968, one was taken from a mist net at Boot Spring (Wauer, 1969*b*). On March 7 and 9, 1976, Philip F. Allan reported hearing two birds calling and observed one by flashlight for five minutes. It may be a winter visitor from the Maderas del Carmen Mountains of Coahuila, Mexico, where it is known to nest (Wauer and Ligon, 1977).

Lesser Nighthawk, *Chordeiles acutipennis*

Goatsuckers:
Family Caprimulgidae

Lesser Nighthawk

Chordeiles acutipennis

Common summer resident and migrant.

It occurs almost everywhere below 4,000 feet in summer, but it is most numerous along the floodplain and in adjacent washes, where its hoarse *purring* can be heard as a low roar at dawn. It does not reach the Big Bend area until April 4 and becomes abundant from mid-April to May 27. On May 25, 1971, I found two eggs beneath a small creosote bush near San Vicente. Summering birds depart by late August, but southbound birds can usually be found along the river until October 18. Migrants have been recorded at Boot Spring and the South Rim. C. Philip Allen observed a flock of 51 individuals north of Persimmon Gap on August 17, 1963.

Common Nighthawk

Chordeiles minor

Uncommon spring migrant (April 22–May 26); rare fall migrant (late July–September 24).

There is no indication that this bird nests within the park, but it is resident in summer north of the park in the Del Norte, Davis, and Glass mountains. After the spring migrants pass through, there are no sightings until July 4, when postnesting birds may be occasional visitors along the river. The fall migration is sparse.

Common Poorwill

Phalaenoptilus nuttallii

Fairly common summer resident; common migrant (April 25–May, early September–October 26); rare in winter.

There are records of this small goatsucker for every month, but only one each for December, January, and February. By the middle of March it can be found along all the park roads below 4,500 feet. In summer it is most common on open desert flats and below the piñon-juniper-oak woodlands, but a few use higher slopes and ridges; I heard poorwills calling from the open, southern side of the Emory Peak ridge

Common Poorwill, *Phalaenoptilus nuttallii*

at 7,000 feet on June 8 and 11, 1968. On October 10, 1970, I counted seven individuals on the road between Panther Junction and Dugout Wells.

Whip-poor-will

Caprimulgus vociferus

Fairly common summer resident (April 2–September 23) in high mountain canyons and along north slopes above 5,700 feet; rare down to 5,300 feet.

Most sightings are from Boot and Pine canyons, but birds can often be heard along the Lost Mine Trail and near Juniper Flat. I found two juveniles and an adult in lower Boot Canyon on June 17, 1971, and Steve Van Pelt discovered a nest with one spotted youngster on a steep oak-covered slope at 5,300 feet on the east side of Ward Mountain, July 19, 1970. Although these birds are very noisy before the breeding period, they are quiet during nestings and by late July may be almost entirely silent except for dusk and dawn songs.

Swifts:
Family Apodidae

Chimney Swift

Chaetura pelagica

Two records for the park.

I observed and heard two individuals calling to one another over Hot Springs on April 27, 1968, and found a lone bird over Rio Grande Village on April 28, 1969. Apparently this species is increasing its range, as I have seen it a number of times in summer in Odessa, Texas. Wolf (1956) regarded it as a summer resident of Texas only as far west as Travis and Bexar counties.

White-throated Swift

Aeronautes saxatalis

Common summer resident and migrant; uncommon in winter.

In summer, it can be found almost anywhere high cliffs exist, from the river canyons to the top of Emory Peak in the Chisos Mountains. It also spends considerable time foraging over the open desert flats. Spring migrants move through the area from late March through May, but fall migrants are less conspicuous, although I saw a flock of 60 to 75 birds over Panther Junction on July 27, 1968. Wintering birds can often be found at the river canyons on mild days. I counted 75 birds at Santa Elena Canyon on December 22, 1967, and 45 near Boquillas

White-throated Swift, *Aeronautes saxatalis*

Canyon on December 30, 1969. This species also has a wintertime roost in a cave under the South Rim.

Hummingbirds:
Family Trochilidae

Broad-billed Hummingbird

Cynanthus latirostris

Five records for the park.

The Broad-billed was first reported by Quillin (1935), who found a nest containing eggs at the Johnson Ranch on May 17, 1934. Mr. and Mrs. Leon Bishop observed one feeding on mountain sage along the Lost Mine Trail on October 20, 1966; and I found one at Boot Canyon on August 7, 1969. Terry Maxwell reported a female "feeding on [tree] tobacco on the river" at the Johnson Ranch, April 20, 1970. And Bill Bouton, Dave Powell, and Vic Reister found a nest containing two young in a side wash off lower Blue Creek Canyon on May 26, 1981.

White-eared Hummingbird

Hylocharis leucotis

Sporadic summer visitor (April 27–September 1) to the Chisos Mountains.

The White-eared Hummingbird appears to have increased in numbers in recent years. During the 1940s, 1950s, and 1960s, it was reported only five times. It was reported ten times from 1972 through 1978, twice in 1980, and twice in 1981. There are no nesting records. A female collected by Tarleton Smith in the Chisos Mountains on July 7, 1937, represents the first Texas record for this species.

Blue-throated Hummingbird

Lampornis clemenciae

Common summer resident (March 30–September 26) in the high Chisos canyons, and uncommon below 5,000 feet.

There also are two sightings of migrants along the river: Roy Hudson saw one at Lajitas on May 22, 1964, and I saw a lone male at Boquillas on April 11, 1969. It is surprisingly common in Boot Canyon in the summer; I counted five pairs along a one-mile stretch on May 9, 1969, and twelve individuals there on August 9, 1969. Birds do not arrive on their nesting grounds until mid-April and depart by late September; I found only three individuals in Boot Canyon on September 19, 1970. Blue-throats utter a loud *seep* that can be heard constantly when they are present. In conrast, the sharp *chip* of the Magnificent Hummer is almost never heard.

Magnificent Hummingbird

Eugenes fulgens

Uncommon summer resident in the higher woodlands of the Chisos Mountains.

It is rarely seen below 6,000 feet, but Pete Koch observed one at Cattail Falls on April 28, 1967. This and the Blue-throated are the two largest of North America's hummers. The male Magnificent has no white in the tail, unlike the Blue-throated. Magnificent Hummers prefer the somewhat higher and drier piñon-juniper-oak woodlands, whereas the Blue-throated is more

Blue-throated Hummingbird, *Lampornis clemenciae*

numerous in the moist canyons and oak zones. Although I have found no proof of nesting, the Magnificent Hummer has been seen regularly from March 30 through August, and it has been reported for the Chisos Mountains since 1955, when Keith L. Dixon found it at Boot Spring on July 21 and 26 (Dixon and Wallmo, 1956).

Lucifer Hummingbird, *Calothorax lucifer*

Lucifer Hummingbird

Calothorax lucifer

Fairly common spring, summer, and fall resident (March 8–November 10); may be sporadic in occurrence.

Joe Kuban's study of hummingbirds in the Chisos Mountains (1977) suggested that Lucifers do better during dry years, when Black-chin numbers are reduced. In May (except on the floodplain, where Black-chins are more plentiful), it may be the hummer most commonly seen from the Rio Grande to the highest slopes of the Chisos Mountains. And when century plants are in bloom, usually from May through September, Lucifers can be found at just about any plant.

Nesting occurs almost anywhere above the low desert and below the forest and woodland habitats in the higher mountains. A nest discovered on a lechuguilla stalk by the Puliches (1963) near Terlingua on July 13, 1962, represented the first nesting record of this species for the United States. Since then, several nests have been found; during May and June 1982, Peter Scott found 24 nests between Panther Junction and the Chisos Basin.

Postnesting birds frequent the mountain canyons; I counted eight males and seven females in Boot Canyon on August 9, 1969. By late August highland birds begin to move into the lowlands, and they can usually be found in the lower canyons until the second week of September, when there is a noticeable decline in sightings. From early October to November they are most often seen in the lower parts of the desert and along the floodplain, where they frequent areas with flowering tree tobacco plants.

Ruby-throated Hummingbird

Archilochus colubris

Rare migrant and postnesting visitor.

There are scattered records from April 30 through October 19, from the Rio Grande floodplain to the Chisos Basin. This species may be more common than the sixteen records suggest; it is next to impossible to identify females in the field, and males are easily overlooked.

Black-chinned Hummingbird

Archilochus alexandri

Common summer resident and migrant.

Black-chins have been recorded every month but January and February. They arrive the second week of March and immediately begin to nest on cottonwoods and mesquites along the river. Two eggs had already hatched in a nest found at Boquillas Crossing, April 18, 1970; the young were ready to leave the nest on May 4 and were gone on May 6 (Wauer). The Black-chin apparently nests throughout the summer; I found a nest with two eggs at Rio Grande Village on June 12, 1970, and a young bird still in the nest in Panther Canyon (4,200 feet in elevation) on August 12, 1967.

Black-chinned Hummingbird, *Archilochus alexandri*

Males begin to move into the Chisos foothills in late March, and by early June, Blackchins can be found at the highest parts of the park. I counted 23 individuals along the Window Trail on July 19, 1969. Their numbers decrease after mid-September, but they can usually be found along the river through December. Like the Lucifer Hummingbird, the Black-chin can often be found at flowering tree tobacco plants. The latest sighting of any year is one by Bill Bromberg at Boquillas on December 28, 1961.

Anna's Hummingbird

Calypte anna

Rare but regular fall migrant and irregular winter visitor.

Borell (1938) first collected one in the Chisos Basin on October 23, 1936, and Lena McBee and Lovie Mae Whitaker found one at Boot Spring on July 24, 1940. There were no other sightings until 1967, when Kent Rylander and I collected an immature male near Santa Elena Canyon on November 5 (Wauer and Rylander, 1968), but it has since been seen several times along the Rio Grande. It remained in the Santa Elena Canyon area throughout December 1967; one was seen on the December 21 Christmas Bird Count. I found four males at Rio Grande Village on November 22, 1969, an immature male near Boquillas Crossing on September 16 and 18, 1970, and two birds on the December 22, 1970, Christmas Bird Count at Rio Grande Village. It apparently overwinters in the area in some years; I discovered one near Boquillas Crossing on February 6, 1968.

Costa's Hummingbird

Calypte costae

Five records for the park.

This little western desert species was seen twice in 1966 and three times in 1983. In 1966, I first discovered a lone male at 7,000 feet on the Lost Mine Trail, August 7, and then Dick Russell and I saw another perched on an ocotillo at Rio Grande Village on December 17. In 1983, all reports were from Rio Grande Village: Anne Bellamy observed a male there on April 12, Debbie Liggett found one on May 2, and Ben Feltner reported one on May 3.

Calliope Hummingbird

Stellula calliope

Seven records for the park.

All records date from August 6 to 22. The Calliope Hummer was first observed in upper Boot Canyon on August 7, 1969, feeding on mountain sage (Wauer). Wesley Cureton next reported one on the Emory Peak Trail, August 9, 1975. Rick LoBello and Marlene Igo found one at a feeder in the Chisos Basin on August 20, 1976; Elton Stilwell reported three or four females near the Pinnacles on August 22, 1978. John and Barbara Ribble found a male at Boot Spring on August 6, 1982, as did Greg Lasley on August 12 and Wendy Watson on August 15.

Broad-tailed Hummingbird, *Selasphorus platycerus*

Broad-tailed Hummingbird

Selasphorus platycercus

Common summer resident of the piñon-juniper-oak woodlands; fairly common migrant.

The Broad-tailed Hummingbird has been recorded every month but January. I have found it along the river as early as February 3, but it does not reach its nesting grounds until late March. I saw an adult male defending a territory at Boot Spring on March 30, 1967, and Julie Hotchkiss and Sharon and Becky Wauer found an adult female feeding two fledged young at Laguna Meadow on May 17, 1969. There is some postnesting movement to the lower slopes of the mountains when century plants begin to bloom in April and May, but mountain sage blossoms become the favorite food source for all the Chisos hummers by July. A high count of 26 Broad-tails was recorded in the vicinity of these red-flowered bushes in Boot Canyon on August 9, 1969 (Wauer).

Hummingbird numbers in the mountains drop off drastically by mid-September, when there is a general exodus throughout the park, except in the floodplain, where there is a slight increase. For the most part, hummingbird sightings in late September through November and as late as December 17 (Wauer) are restricted to tree tobacco stands along the river.

Rufous Hummingbird

Selasphorus rufus

Rare migrant in spring and common in late summer and fall.

This is the first of the fall migrants to arrive in the mountains, appearing as early as July 20 and becoming abundant at flower-covered slopes by early August. Charles Bender counted more than fifty Rufous Hummers along the South Rim Trail on August 19, 1966. Like other mountain hummers, the Rufous prefers mountain sage to century plants. Its numbers decrease considerably by mid-September, but a few specimens can usually be found at flowering mountain sages until October 23. It has been recorded along the river through December 22. Springtime sightings are few: Mr. and Mrs. A. L. Rawls saw one near Burro Mesa Pouroff on February 7, 1967, and I observed one at Rio Grande Village on March 7, 1967.

Rufous Hummingbird, *Selasphorus rufus*

Allen's Hummingbird

Selasphorus sasin

Rare postnesting visitor (August 6–October 5).

There is one early report of a male on the Window Trail, May 18, 1978, by Margaret Littlejohn. This is an extremely difficult bird to identify after nesting and care must be taken not to confuse it with immature Rufous Hummers.

Trogons:
Family Trogonidae

Elegant Trogon

Trogon elegans

Extremely rare visitor.

There were several sightings of a female Elegant Trogon within the Chisos Basin from early January to mid-April 1980. It was first reported along the lower Window Trail on January 8 by Ronald Tibball and party; Norman Scott and Hope Spear found it that day also. The next day, Jerry and Nancy Strickling and Jim Shiflett saw it in the same vicinity. K. H. Husmann next reported it near the Chisos Mountains Lodge on February 10 and C. L. Sackett, Jr., reported it near the cottages on March 9 and 16. It was last seen near Boulder Meadow on April 15 by Patricia Collins and Stephanie Frederick.

There are two earlier records for the park. Sue Corson first reported one near the Basin sewage lagoons on May 9, 1969, and David Cox reported a female from Boot Spring on August 29, 1972.

Kingfishers:
Family Alcedinidae

Belted Kingfisher

Ceryle alcyon

Fairly common migrant and rare winter visitor.

It has been recorded every month but June; there is an absence of records only from May 14 to July 9. I have found no evidence of nesting, but some years this bird reaches the Big Bend in early July, and individuals remain at ponds and appropriate stretches of the Rio Grande for several months. Migrants are most common along the river, but I found a lone bird at Panther Junction on April 6, 1969, and one at 6,600 feet in Boot Canyon on September 28, 1969. Most sightings are of one or two individuals, but I recorded six at Rio Grande Village on October 3, 1968.

Green Kingfisher

Chloroceryle americana

Uncommon spring and summer visitor (March 29–October 27) to the ponds at Rio Grande Village.

There is no evidence of nesting. Apparently this species has increased its range in the last two decades; there are no records before 1966.

Woodpeckers:
Family Picidae

Lewis' Woodpecker

Melanerpes lewis

Four park records.

Sutton (1935) collected one at Boot Spring on May 1, 1935; Joseph and Harriet Woolfenden observed one at Rio Grande Village in January 1963; I found one flying over Boot Canyon on October 22, 1968; and Jimmie Stovall and Doug Evans observed one at Panther Junction on October 30, 1982.

Red-headed Woodpecker

Melanerpes erythrocephalus

Seven records for the park.

The earliest record is for April 3 (one in Maple Canyon by J. Adkins in 1974); the latest is for July 27 (one in the Chisos Basin by Tarleton Smith in 1936). Three of the seven records are from the lowlands at Rio Grande Village.

Acorn Woodpecker, *Melanerpes formicivorus*

Acorn Woodpecker

Melanerpes formicivorus

Common resident of the Chisos woodlands; abundant at Boot Spring.

The Acorn Woodpecker is most numerous in the upper canyons and ranges to the lower edge of the oaks in late summer and fall. There are also several records made a considerable distance from the mountain woodlands: G. V. Oliver and J. M. Fitzgerald reported one at Dugout Wells on May 18, 1975; Esequiel Richard found one at Panther Junction on July 11, 1977; Elton and Brad Stilwell observed one at Rio Grande Village on August 19, 1978; and I found one among the mesquites at Solis on November 11, 1967. There are several nesting records, all in live oaks or piñons from early May through July. The easiest place to find this bird is within the canyon along the north side of the Basin Campground.

Golden-fronted Woodpecker

Melanerpes aurifrons

Rare spring migrant; rare nesting bird along the river.

The status of this bird has changed recently. Before 1970, it was considered a rare spring migrant (April 2 to May 13), and there were two fall sightings: one at Boquillas on September 10, 1955 (National Park Service files), and one at 5,900 feet on the Lost Mine Trail on November 6, 1966 (Wauer). During the 1970s, there was a single record: Frank Deckert observed one female at Panther Junction on January 2, 1978.

From late 1981 through 1983, however, there were twice as many sightings as there had been previously. What's more, nesting has been reported for Rio Grande Village, Dugout Wells,

Panther Junction, and possibly Cottonwood Campground. Apparently, the species has discovered the available habitats within the park. The nearest previously known nesting sites were at Calamity Creek, just south of Alpine, and at The Post, a park just south of Marathon.

Yellow-bellied Sapsucker

Sphyrapicus varius

Uncommon migrant and fairly common winter resident.

Records range from September 23 to March 29, and there is a late sighting of a lone bird at Rio Grande Village, following a period of stormy weather, on May 3, 1969 (Wauer). It occurs throughout the wooded parts of the park in winter but is most easily found at areas of cottonwoods in the lowlands, such as Rio Grande Village and Cottonwood Campground. Migrants usually are found singly, but I found twenty or more birds on October 25, 1967, at Rio Grande Village.

Williamson's Sapsucker

Sphyrapicus thyroideus

Sporadic migrant and winter visitor.

It was first recorded by Richard D. Porter, who collected one in Pine Canyon on October 18, 1957. There were no further reports until the 1967–68 winter, when it was seen on a number of occasions from October 28 through February 23. I did not see it at all during my six years' residency as chief park naturalist (1966–72), although Maurice Mackey reported one on the Lost Mine Trail on November 26, 1970, and Jim

Tucker found one at Laguna Meadow on December 29 the same year. After this, there were no reports of the bird until 1979, when Mark Beaman found two males at Boot Canyon on November 26, and Jean Nance observed one at Laguna Meadow. There was one 1980 report: Robert and Sean DeVine found one at Panther Junction on October 21. Gard Otis reported a male from Laguna Meadow on September 16, 1981, and R. A. Wolinski observed a female in Pine Canyon on March 10, 1983. Bonnie McKinney reported one near the Basin Amphitheatre on November 18, 1983.

Ladder-backed Woodpecker

Picoides scalaris

Common resident below 6,000 feet and irregular postnesting visitor above.

This is the common woodpecker of the Chihuahuan Desert. I have found it nesting in cottonwoods, willows, oaks, piñon pines, century plant stalks, utility poles, and wooden signposts. Totals of 22, 16, 32, 24, and 34 were found on the Rio Grande Village and Chisos Mountains Christmas Counts from 1966 through 1970, respectively.

Northern Flicker

Colaptes auratus

Uncommon summer resident in the Chisos highlands; common migrant and winter resident.

Big Bend's breeding flicker is of special interest because it represents the northern breeding population of the Mexican race of the red-shafted form, which is resident in the United States only in the Chisos Mountains. Adult birds were discovered feeding young at a nest twelve feet high in a dead ponderosa pine snag near Boot Spring on May 8, 1968 (Wauer). By early July, postnesting birds disperse into lower elevations and can be found in the Basin and Green Gulch.

Flickers are most numerous in migration from late February to April 23, and September 24 through November. Migrants and wintering birds can be expected anywhere, although they are most common below 5,600 feet.

All of the above applies to the red-shafted birds, although yellow-shafted birds are considered rare in migration and sporadic in winter. Records range from mid-October through March, and the vast majority of sightings are from the lowlands near the Rio Grande; sightings of the yellow-shafted birds at higher elevations are rare.

Tyrant Flycatchers: *Family Tyrannidae*

Olive-sided Flycatcher

Contopus borealis

Fairly common migrant (April 4–June 8, August 4–October 4).

It is most numerous in the mountains but occurs regularly along the river and over the desert as well. I counted nineteen individuals in the Chisos Mountains May 12 through 15, 1967.

Greater Pewee

Contopus pertinax

Rare migrant in spring and fall; two winter sightings.

There are four spring sightings: I heard one calling its very distinct *ho-say Maria* song above Laguna Meadow on June 8, 1968; Ted Parker and Harold Morrin heard and saw one just above Juniper Flat on May 29, 1971; Bobby Fredericks reported two in the Chisos Basin on May 29, 1973; and Larry and Martha Ballard, Shirley Wright, and Amos Adkins reported one at Panther Junction on May 29, 1980. There are also four fall sightings: I observed one at the South Rim on September 4, 1977; Morgan Jones and Steve Hawkins reported one at Rio Grande Village on September 3, 1978; and Bonnie McKinney reported one at Rio Grande Village on September 12, 1983. Both winter sightings were made at Cottonwood Campground: Jerry and Nancy Strickling reported one on December 21, 1974, and William and Alice Roe reported one there on January 6, 1975.

Western Wood-Pewee

Contopus sordidulus

Common migrant in the park; breeds in the Davis Mountains.

Pansy Espy reported that it "nests every summer" in the Davis Mountains; she photographed a nest built in May 1970. On June 12 and 27 and July 13, 1971, I found a lone individual vigorously singing and defending a territory within the Rio Grande Village Campground. Spring records begin with very early sightings at Rio Grande Village on March 3, 1967 (Russ and Marian Wilson), and near Persimmon Gap on March 15, 1971 (Wauer), followed by a lapse in sightings until April 13, when the bulk of northbound migrants reach the Big Bend. The spring movement continues through June 12 and reaches a peak between April 25 and May 18, when the bird may be found almost anywhere from the river to the top of the Chisos Mountains. Postnesting birds may reach the park as early as July 16. Fall migrants are common from August 6 to mid-September, and the peak is followed by a trickle of southbound birds, particularly within the mountains, until October 30.

Yellow-bellied Flycatcher

Empidonax flaviventris

Two records for the park.

I took specimens in lower Pine Canyon on September 3, 1968, and at Rio Grande Village on September 1, 1969. Since this bird is easily overlooked, it may be more common in fall than the records indicate.

Willow Flycatcher

Empidonax traillii

Rare summer resident; uncommon spring migrant (May 11–May 28); fairly common fall migrant (July 21–September 24).

Traill's Flycatcher was split by the revised AOU *Check-list* (1983) into this species (the *fitz-bew* singer) and the Alder Flycatcher (*Empidonax alnorum*). Since the Alder Flycatcher is a northern bird that does not occur in the park, all the records can be considered together.

Specimens were taken at Grapevine Spring on July 21, 1956 (Texas A&M University), at a tank near Panther Junction on June 14, 1968 (David Easterla), and at Rio Grande Village on August 25, 1967 (Wauer).

Least Flycatcher

Empidonax minimus

Uncommon spring migrant (April 20–May 29) and common fall migrant (July 21–October 10).

It has been recorded at all elevations but is most numerous in the lowlands. Specimens taken include four in September at various elevations and one in the Chisos Basin on May 3, 1967 (Wauer).

Hammond's Flycatcher

Empidonax hammondii

Fairly common spring migrant (March 24–May 17); rare in fall (August 24–September 20).

It has been recorded at all elevations but is most numerous in the mountains. Specimens were taken from the Chisos Basin on March 24, 1935, from Laguna Meadow on May 3, 1935, from Boot Canyon on May 6 and 7, 1932, from Pine Canyon on May 9 and 14, 1933 (Van Tyne and Sutton, 1937), from Boquillas Crossing on April 12, 1967, and from Rio Grande Village on September 6, 1968 (Wauer), and September 20, 1957 (Richard D. Porter).

Dusky Flycatcher

Empidonax oberholseri

Fairly common spring migrant (April 22–May 17); sporadic in winter.

There is also one fall sighting, at Castolon on September 15, 1969 (Wauer). During the first two weeks of May the Dusky Flycatcher may be numerous within the Chisos woodlands and rare along the river. There are several records made along the floodplain during the winters of 1968–69 and 1970–71, but I did not find it other winters. Specimens were taken from Maple Canyon on May 2, 1967, from Laguna Meadow on May 4, 1967, from Boot Spring on May 9, 1969, from Green Gulch on May 16, 1968, and from Santa Elena Canyon on December 30, 1968 (Wauer).

Gray Flycatcher

Empidonax wrightii

Uncommon spring migrant (April 3–June 6); one fall record.

There is a single fall sighting of one bird at Boot Spring on August 29, 1970 (David Easterla and Jim Tucker). Most spring records are from the mountains, but I found lone birds at Rio Grande Village on April 8, 1968, April 8, 1970, and April 3, 1971. Van Tyne and Sutton (1937) reported taking specimens in the Chisos Basin April 26 and 27, 1935, at Pine Canyon on May 1, 1933, and in the Chisos Mountains May 5 through 23, 1932.

Western Flycatcher

Empidonax difficilis

Common only in Boot Canyon in summer; rare migrant.

Records range from April 1 through October 5. It arrives on its nesting grounds in mid-April and remains until late August. Nests are built on cliffs and overhangs along the drainage; I found nest-building on June 10, 1969, and fledged birds on July 19. David Wolf found an adult feeding young at Boot Spring on August 22, 1968. Fall migrants were seen in the Chisos Basin on October 4, 1968; a specimen was taken in Pine Canyon on September 7, 1955 (Texas A&M University). Lone birds were found at Dugout Wells on September 11, 1967, and September 11, 1968 (Wauer). It has been recorded only once along the river; I observed a lone bird at Rio Grande Village on April 1, 1969.

Black Phoebe, *Sayornis nigricans*

Black Phoebe

Sayornis nigricans

Fairly common resident along the river; rare migrant.

Nest-building was found inside the motel ruins at Hot Springs on March 26, 1969; a Say's Phoebe was building a nest not more than fifty feet away. Although the Black Phoebe can usually be found easily before nesting, one must often search for it during the nesting period.

Soon after mid-July, however, adults and young appear everywhere along the river and at adjacent ponds. Migrants are few and far between but pass through the area from mid-March to April 11 and from early August through September. Sightings are all from the vicinity of the river, except one for the Old Sam Nail Ranch on September 9, 1966 (Wauer), and one at Boot Spring on August 10, 1970 (Walter Boles, Jim Shields, and John St. Julien).

Eastern Phoebe

Sayornis phoebe

Fairly common winter resident (October 8–April 1) along the river.

I have found it regularly at Rio Grande Village and Cottonwood Campground each winter.

Say's Phoebe

Sayornis saya

Fairly common in summer; common migrant and winter resident.

Some birds are permanent residents; I have banded and recaptured birds at Panther Junction throughout the year. Breeding birds begin to nest in mid-March. In 1968, a pair nested in the deserted Daniels house at Rio Grande Village in April and again in July; fledged birds were seen on May 10 and August 6. Young birds left a nest at Panther Junction on July 7, 1970 (Wauer). There is some postnesting movement into the highlands, where birds can be seen up to 7,200 feet. Migrants pass through the area from mid-March through mid-May and during September and October. Although most of the migrant Say's Phoebes pass through the lowlands, occasional birds are found in Boot Canyon, along the Lost Mine Trail, and at other highland areas. From early November through April, however, there are no sightings above 5,500 feet.

Vermilion Flycatcher, *Pyrocephalus rubinus*

Vermilion Flycatcher

Pyrocephalus rubinus

Common summer resident, fairly common winter resident at localized areas along the river, and common migrant.

Nest-building was found on cottonwoods at Rio Grande Village on three occasions: during the second week of March 1971; on March 23, 1968; and on May 10, 1968 (Wauer). The 1968 nests were 5 and 35 feet above the ground, respectively. I observed an adult male feeding a fledged youngster as late as August 1, 1967.

The Vermilion Flycatcher is most common as a spring migrant from March 7 through mid-April, when it may be found up to 4,000 feet. Harold Brodrick found one at Dagger Flat on March 9, 1956, and it regularly visits Panther Junction from March 7 to March 25. There apparently is some postnesting movement along the river and into the lowlands, as Dick Rasp found one at Oak Spring on July 12, 1964; however, most of the breeding birds remain on their nesting grounds until late September. During early October the Vermilion Flycatcher may become rare at Rio Grande Village, but by the third week of October another wave of migrants seems to boost the population considerably. I have found it regularly at Rio Grande Village (but nowhere else within the park) during December, January, and February, except in the winter of 1969–70. Some winters it can be found at Cottonwood Campground as well. There are also two sightings of this bird in the Chisos Mountains: Margaret Littlejohn reported lone birds near the Basin Ranger Station on March 29 and April 6, 1978.

Dusky-capped Flycatcher

Myiarchus tuberculifer

Rare migrant and postnesting visitor.

A specimen collected by Van Tyne and Sutton (1937) at Glenn Spring, June 17, 1932, represents the first for Texas. It has since been reported a number of times from April 17 through July 7, most often in the Chisos woodlands. There is no evidence of nesting, although I found three singing birds in Boot Canyon on May 8 and 9, 1970. And there are two additional park records: I found three birds at Rio Grande Village on October 23, 1968, and David Pashley reported one at Rio Grande Village with "song distinct" on December 12, 1977.

Ash-throated Flycatcher

Myiarchus cinerascens

Common summer resident; common spring migrant; uncommon fall migrant; sporadic in winter.

From mid-March through July 26 this is one of the most numerous birds of the Big Bend area. It nests along the river floodplain, at springs, in arroyos within the desert, and upward into the highest parts of the piñon-juniper woodlands. By the last of July, however, summering birds leave their breeding grounds. They then become uncommon, except for occasional migrants along the river and in the desert washes. Although in other parts of the Southwest these birds gather in family groups after nesting, the majority of the fall migrants that pass through the Big Bend until late September are alone.

Wintering birds occur rather sporadically. Two or three individuals can sometimes be found at cottonwood and mesquite groves in the lowlands. I found this bird at Rio Grande Village and near Castolon regularly during the winters of 1966–67, 1967–68, and 1968–69, but only twice during December, January, and February, 1969–70.

Great Crested Flycatcher

Myiarchus crinitus

Rare fall visitor (August 24–October 29) along the river floodplain.

There were no records of this eastern *Myiarchus* for the park prior to 1968, but after that I found it regularly. All three specimens collected (at Castolon on September 15, 1969, and

Ash-throated Flycatcher, *Myiarchus cinerascens*

at Rio Grande Village on September 16, 1970, and September 28, 1968) have been juveniles.

Brown-crested Flycatcher

Myiarchus tyrannulus

Rare migrant and vagrant.

Records range from March 10 through September 13. There is no evidence of nesting, although it does nest in the lower Rio Grande Valley and in southern New Mexico. It is likely that the majority of the late summer and fall birds are postnesting vagrants. I found six individuals at Cottonwood Campground on May 26, 1968.

Sulphur-bellied Flycatcher

Myiodynastes luteiventris

Three records for the park.

On May 11, 1969, Jim Tucker, Doug Eddleman, and I found a lone bird at Rio Grande Village. Glenn Lowe, Jr., found one at Boulder Meadow on August 5, 1973. Ruth Snyder reported one just below Laguna Meadow on May 9, 1976.

Tropical Kingbird

Tyrannus melancholicus

Couch's Kingbird

Tyrannus couchii

Rare migrant and postnesting bird (April 27–October 9).

The 1983 AOU *Check-list* split the former

Tropical Kingbird into these two species. Since field differentiations are extremely difficult with these two forms, and all previous records have been kept together, they will be considered together here. However, all future records should be kept separate whenever possible.

There are records of nest-building. During the summer of 1971, I found a lone bird defending a territory and nest-building on a cottonwood at Rio Grande Village; it remained in the area near the lake behind the store from June 22 through August 4. As far as I could determine, it remained alone but continued vigorously to defend a territory. I have recorded Tropical Kingbirds on a number of occasions in the fall; one of three birds seen at Cottonwood Campground on September 2, 1968, was collected and was identified as *couchii* by Allan Phillips.

Cassin's Kingbird

Tyrannus vociferans

Rare summer resident and uncommon migrant; two winter records.

There are one or two nesting records at Rio Grande Village and Cottonwood Campground almost every year. Cassin's Kingbird is much more common north of the park, along Calamity and Limpia creeks and in the Davis Mountains. Early spring migrants reach the Big Bend area as early as March 10 and have been recorded as late as mid-May. Fall migrants trickle through the area from mid-July to the last of October; I found three at Panther Junction on the evening of September 29, 1970.

Thick-billed Kingbird

Tyrannus crassirostris

Rare spring visitor (March 20–May 25); one summer record; rare in fall and early winter (September 30–December 28).

The first Texas record is of a lone bird found in the Chisos Basin by Michel and O. R. Henderson on June 21, 1967 (Wauer, 1967*e*). It remained for about three hours near the sewage lagoons, where it was photographed by the Hendersons, and Dick Nelson and I observed it. On December 23, 1970, I found one on the mesquite flats near Boquillas Canyon. It remained in the vicinity throughout the winter. Mrs. James Owen observed it in late February 1971; Captain and Mrs. E. B. Hurlbert, Becky Wauer, and I observed it on March 20; and David Easterla and Dave Snyder saw it on April 5. A Thick-billed was not seen again until May 25, when I found a lone bird on the floodplain at San Vicente Crossing. Al Crockett found one at Rio Grande Village on December 28, 1973. Bonnie McKinney reported one near La Linda on April 1, 1982, and one at Persimmon Gap Ranger Station on September 30, 1983.

Western Kingbird

Tyrannus verticalis

Rare summer resident; fairly common spring migrant (April 1–May 27); uncommon in fall.

Western Kingbirds nested on cottonwoods at Panther Junction during June and July 1968 and 1969, on a willow next to the river at Rio Grande Village in June 1970, and on a tall cottonwood in the Rio Grande Village Campground in the summer of 1971. Nest-building was found on June 22, adults were feeding young on July 13, and a fledged youngster was seen there on August 4 (Wauer). Spring migrants reach a peak from April 28 to May 17. Most sightings are from the floodplain, but this species has been seen almost everywhere below the Chisos woodlands. Fall migrants are few and far between and have been recorded as late as October 12. Most sightings are of lone birds, but family groups of three to five birds are occasionally recorded.

Eastern Kingbird

Tyrannus tyrannus

Rare spring and fall migrant (May 13–June 28, August 24–September 18); one winter record.

The winter sighting was made on February 18, 1977, at Rio Grande Village by Josephine Potter. All reports are from below 4,000 feet.

Scissor-tailed Flycatcher

Tyrannus forficatus

Uncommon migrant (April 8–late June, August 12–October 18).

All sightings were made below 4,000 feet. This is a fairly common breeding bird north of the park near Marathon and to the north and east.

Rose-throated Becard

Pachyramphus aglaiae

Five records for the park.

Richard B. Starr, who saw three males and

two females in a flock at the Santa Elena Canyon picnic site on September 24, 1965, was the first to report this species. Craig Booth next reported one at Santa Elena Crossing on April 26, 1975. The other three reports are from the Chisos Basin: Jim and Nathalie Baines reported one male and two females near the campground on February 26, 1976; Ira Taylor found one male near the lagoons on October 22, 1979; and M. F. Marchase reported a female near the lagoons on February 7, 1982.

Larks:
Family Alaudidae

Horned Lark

Eremophila alpestris

Uncommon migrant and rare winter visitor in the park; common all year on the open grasslands near Marathon and north to Fort Stockton.

It has been reported for the park every month but July, August, and September, but I have not found it regularly anywhere. Most park observations are of small flocks of three and four birds along the River Road, on Tornillo Flat, or in the Chisos Basin.

Swallows:
Family Hirundinidae

Purple Martin

Progne subis

Five records for the park.

It was first reported from a specimen taken at San Vicente on May 20, 1935, by Van Tyne and Sutton (1937). Smith (1935) found three in lower Green Gulch on June 11, 1935. Alexander Sprunt, Jr., and John H. Dick reported one at Hot Springs on July 24, 1951. Bert and Millie Schaughency saw one there on April 22, 1971, and David Easterla reported one female at Rio Grande Village on August 17, 1972.

Tree Swallow

Tachycineta bicolor

Uncommon spring migrant (March 4–May 1) along the river; rare in fall (July 31–September 9); two winter reports.

David and Karl Wiedenfeld and Ed Gildenwater found thirteen individuals along the river at Rooney's Place on December 29, 1977; Adele West reported it at Rio Grande Village on January 17, 1963.

Violet-green Swallow

Tachycineta thalassina

Uncommon summer resident in the Chisos Mountains; fairly common spring migrant; rare fall migrant.

This species begins to move along the Rio Grande as early as February 24 and may become regular along the river by the first of March. It does not reach its nesting grounds in the mountains until March 17. The movement of spring migrants continues along the river and occasionally over the desert until May 3. Nesting birds utilize cliffs above 5,200 feet in Green Gulch, in the Basin, in upper Juniper and Pine canyons, and on Emory Peak. By the second week of July, nesting apparently completed, the birds move elsewhere; there are few records for the park from July 7 through most of August. Southbound migrants begin to appear along the river by the last few days of August. The fall migration is sparse but extends through October. There is also a single winter sighting of two birds at Rio Grande Village, December 28, 1965, by Raymond Fleetwood.

Northern Rough-winged Swallow

Stelgidopteryx serripennis

Fairly common summer resident; common spring migrant; uncommon in fall and winter along the river.

It is most numerous from mid-February through May, when northbound migrants are passing through the area and breeding birds are nesting. Two pairs of Rough-wings were seen carrying nesting materials into holes in a mud bank at Solis on February 21, 1969 (Wauer). Sightings continue throughout the summer at localized areas along the river, such as Hot Springs, Solis, and Castolon. There is only a slight increase in numbers in late September as fall migrants move along the waterways. Wintering birds can usually be found in small flocks of three to a dozen along the Rio Grande. Combined Christmas Counts at Castolon and Rio Grande Village were 29, 61, 60, 26, and 42 in 1966 through 1970, respectively.

Bank Swallow

Riparia riparia

Uncommon spring migrant (February 24–May 20) along the river; rare fall migrant (August 17–September 1); one winter sighting.

On December 8, 1967, I saw a lone bird at Rio Grande Village. Like the Tree Swallow, this species is never common but can be found with other migrating swallows at appropriate times of the year.

Cliff Swallow, *Hirundo pyrrhonota*

Cliff Swallow

Hirundo pyrrhonota

Common summer resident along the river and less numerous in the desert; uncommon migrant.

It arrives as early as March 20 and begins to nest immediately. Nests can be found on cliffs adjacent to the river throughout the canyons and at other appropriate places. Early birds also reach bridges and cliffs a considerable distance from the river; several were seen nest-building in Boquillas Canyon on March 22, 1969, and I found twelve individuals at nests on the upper Tornillo Creek bridge on March 25, 1968. It apparently nests on cliffs in rather inhospitable places during wet years; I found several places on Tornillo Flat where Cliff Swallow nests had been constructed earlier but were not in use at the time. C. Philip Allen searched for Cliff Swallow nests in 1963 and reported 53 at the upper Tornillo Creek bridge, 55 at Hot Springs, 8 at the bridge west of Castolon, and 21 at Devil's Den.

The bulk of the nesting birds leave their first breeding grounds by mid-July, but there apparently is a second nesting some years. I found occupied nests under the bridges at Nine Point Draw and upper Tornillo Creek during August 1970. Lone birds or small flocks of migrants can be expected along the river until mid-October, and a flock of seven birds was sighted at Hot Springs on October 20, 1967 (Wauer).

Cave Swallow

Hirundo fulva

One small colony known to nest in the park.

Don Davis first found nests of this species in the twilight part of a cave along the eastern slope of Mariscal Mountain in January 1969. On May 27, he and I visited this area and found a total of 13 Cave Swallows using two caves; there were three active nests. Cliff Swallows were nesting near the entrance of one cave. On July 17, David Easterla found 20 to 25 birds at the caves and three more active nests. Cave Swallows were found nesting there again in May and July 1970. This species is rare in migration, but I have found it at Castolon on August 16, 1969, and April 4, 1970, and at Rio Grande Village on September 14, 1968 (25 to 30 individuals), October 5, 1969, and April 18, 1970.

Barn Swallow

Hirundo rustica

Summer resident at a few localized places; fairly common migrant (March 2–late May, early August–November 5).

The earliest arrival date at Panther Junction is March 24. Nesting occurs on buildings at Rio Grande Village, Castolon, Panther Junction, and the Basin. The first young are usually fledged by late June; young left the nest at the Rio Grande Village store on June 26, 1968. A second clutch is usually produced in August; nestlings were banded at Panther Junction on September 11, 1966, and September 2, 1968. It is most numerous in migration, and flocks of fifteen to fifty birds can be found along the river; it has also been seen over the desert and high in the Chisos Mountains.

Jays, Ravens, Nutcrackers: *Family Corvidae*

Steller's Jay

Cyanocitta stelleri

Sporadic winter visitor (November 13–April 17).

The November 13 sighting was made near Boulder Meadow in 1972 by Mr. and Mrs. Don Troyer, the April 17 observation by K. C. Cummings and W. C. Matthews at Boot Spring in 1973 (fifteen to twenty individuals). There were no records of this bird in the park before March 16, 1970, when Mrs. Campbell Steketee saw one bird at the South Rim. It is resident in the highland forest of the Davis Mountains.

Blue Jay

Cyanocitta cristata

Rare winter visitor and vagrant.

It was first reported for the park by Harold Brodrick, who found it at Panther Junction on November 2, 1956. One stayed at Castolon from December 30, 1967, to February 6, 1968 (Jim Court and Wauer). It was next reported, again at Castolon, from February 3 (G. Maisel) to April 21 (Doris and Julian Darden) in 1976. Bert and Millie Schaughency and Dean Amadon reported one at Rio Grande Village on April 29, 1977. And there were two 1982 reports: one bird at Rio Grande Village on June 1 by Bruce and Chris Palmer, and two birds at Black Gap Wildlife Management Area headquarters on October 24 by Bonnie McKinney.

Scrub Jay

Aphelocoma coerulescens

Sporadic in occurrence in recent years.

The Scrub Jay was first recorded in the park as a lone bird in Green Gulch on December 28, 1967 (Wauer). It was next seen in 1976 from February 4 (four to six birds in the Basin by G. Maisel) through May 18 ("some below the Basin Campground" by Randy Koroter), then at Laguna Meadow on November 7 (Rick LoBello); a pair was sighted at the Basin Campground on December 15 (Peter Scott). It was not reported again until 1979: Robert Harms found several along the Window Trail on January 4; LoBello heard and saw one in Blue Creek Canyon on March 20; and David Wolf and Rose Ann Rowlett reported three at the start of the Laguna Meadow Trail in the Basin on April 20. This species is common north of the park in the Del Norte and Davis mountains.

Gray-breasted Jay

Aphelocoma ultramarina

Common resident in the piñon-juniper-oak woodlands in the Chisos Mountains.

This is one of the most conspicuous birds of the mountains, and flocks of 5 to 18 are common. Christmas counters recorded 25 in 1966, 222 in 1967, 180 in 1968, 18 in 1969, and 106 in 1970. Nesting occurs during April, May, and June; nests were found on a Grave's oak near Laguna Meadow on May 8, 1970, and on an Emory oak near the Window on May 11, 1968 (Wauer); and C. Philip Allen reported fledged birds at Boot Spring on June 1, 1963. There

Gray-breasted Jay, *Aphelocoma ultramarina*

apparently is some local movement to lower elevations during some winters. One was seen in upper Big Brushy Canyon, in the northern part of the Dead Horse Mountains, on October 13, 1969, and one was found at Rio Grande Village on December 13, 1969 (Wauer).

The Gray-breasted Jay is the only resident jay of the Chisos and Maderas del Carmen mountains, although there are habitats suitable for Steller's and Scrub Jays. It appears that the Gray-breasted Jay is dominant wherever it occurs.

Clark's Nutcracker

Nucifraga columbiana

Four reports for the park.

John Galley (1951) was the first to find one, on the Lost Mine Trail on October 16, 1950. Mr. and Mrs. Forrest Roulands found five there on October 30, 1966. Paul and Carol Krausman and John and Mary Bissonette reported one feeding in their yard at Panther Junction on November 19, 1972. And E. Kendall and L. Feazel reported one in upper Juniper Canyon on February 28, 1979.

Chihuahuan Raven

Corvus cryptoleucus

Rare summer visitor and migrant in the lower part of the Big Bend; common on the mesquite flats in the northern part of Brewster County and north into New Mexico.

Although this species is generally considered to be resident over most of its range, I have found it to move into the northern Big Bend area during March and April. Nests can be found on mesquites and utility poles along the highways between Marathon and Sanderson and west toward Marfa. The status of this raven in the park has apparently changed in recent years. Van Tyne and Sutton (1937) reported it as common, but I have found it only irregularly, and there are no records for February. Most of the recent park sightings are from Tornillo Flat and south to the lower Tornillo Creek bridge. The majority of these records are of one or two individuals, but David Simon found a flock of six on August 30, 1967.

Common Raven

Corvus corax

Fairly common resident from the Rio Grande to the top of the Chisos Mountains.

This is the common raven throughout the park; Chihuahuan Ravens are only occasionally seen in the desert lowlands. Common Ravens nest in early spring. One nest was reported in Hot Springs Canyon on April 12, 1983 (Bruce Talbot); young were fledged from a nest on Tornillo Flat in mid-April 1968; and adults were feeding young in a nest in lower Hot Springs Canyon on May 4, 1970 (Wauer). T. and B. Alex reported two adults and two fledglings at Hot Springs on June 12, 1983.

Postnesting birds residing near the mountains roost in the highlands and move into the desert to feed each morning. They can often be found soaring over mountain ridges and peaks in the afternoons: 43 birds were seen over the South Rim on May 10, 1969, and 32 were seen circling over Boot Canyon on October 22, 1967 (Wauer). Frank Deckert reported a flock of 65 flying northward over Panther Junction on October 26, 1979. In winter, more than 40 individuals commonly use a deep cut in the cliff near Boot Canyon Pouroff as a nightly roost.

Common Raven, *Corvus corax*

Titmice:
Family Paridae

Tufted Titmouse

Parus bicolor

Common resident of the Chisos Mountains.

Nesting occurs during April, May, and June; nest-building was found at Juniper Spring on May 1, 1932 (Van Type and Sutton, 1937), and at Juniper Flat on May 20, 1967, and adults

Tufted Titmouse, *Parus bicolor*

were seen feeding young at Boot Spring on June 11, 1967 (Wauer). It occasionally wanders into the lowlands. There are several sightings of lone birds at Rio Grande Village: I found birds there from November 11 to December 12, 1969; David Wolf reported an immature bird there on September 7, 1973; and J. Speer found one there on January 6, 1983. The 1983 AOU *Check-list* lumped the Tufted Titmouse with the Black-crested Titmouse, the name previously used for the variety found in the Big Bend.

Verdin:
Family Remizidae

Verdin

Auriparus flaviceps

Fairly common resident in the desert lowlands up to 4,000 feet.

This little bird can be difficult to find, but a search along the lowland washes and at mesquite thickets along the river is sure to produce one or more. Nesting seems to be most common in April, May, and June, but late summer nesting is not unusual. There is some postnesting wandering; I found one individual at Laguna Meadow on October 18, 1969. Wintertime nest-building does not mean that the bird is breeding then.

Bushtit:
Family Aegithalidae

Bushtit

Psaltriparus minimus

Common resident above the lower edge of the piñon-juniper-oak woodlands.

This species includes both the black-eared and the plain phases, which are regarded in earlier publications as two species. Studies of the bird in Mexico, Arizona, New Mexico, and the Big Bend area have proven that most of the black-eared birds are merely juvenile males. Some breeding males, however, may possess the black-eared coloration; I found a black-eared bird mounting a plain bird near the Window on March 19, 1967. It is also possible to see black-eared birds feeding plain birds and vice versa. Adults have been found to lay a second clutch of eggs before the first young have left the family; thus fledged birds may actually help feed their younger brothers and sisters. Additional information about the color phases in these birds can be obtained by reading Phillips, Marshall, and Monson (1964, 111–113) and Raitt (1967).

During most of the year, Bushtits occur in flocks ranging from small family groups of 8 to 10 birds to groups of 45 and 55 individuals.

Verdin, *Auriparus flaviceps*

Then they are easy to locate because they constantly call to one another as they move through the woodlands feeding upon insects. Their calls may be heard from as far away as two hundred feet. During the nesting season, they may be rather difficult to find because they are usually quiet when incubating or feeding young. Nests have been found from mid-March to early June, usually with difficulty, because they are placed in dense foliage of junipers and pines; one nest was found among mistletoe on a drooping juniper in Boot Canyon on May 8, 1968 (Wauer). As the season progresses, there are fewer black-eared birds, although right after nesting, a flock may consist of half black-eared and half plain birds.

Nuthatches:
Family Sittidae

Red-breasted Nuthatch

Sitta canadensis

Sporadic migrant and winter visitor.

This bird is common some years but completely absent others. Records range from September 16 (one reported by Vicki Glen from the East Rim in 1982) through the winter to May 3 (a pair reported for Boot Canyon by Walter Ellison and Richard Prum in 1979). All of the reports are from the Chisos Mountains except for three sightings at Rio Grande Village on October 14, 1955 (John Palmer), October 29, 1967 (Wauer), and October 25, 1976 (Connie Snapp).

White-breasted Nuthatch

Sitta carolinensis

Fairly common resident in the upper woodlands of the Chisos Mountains.

In summer it can best be found at Laguna Meadow or in Boot Canyon among stands of tall cypress or pines. There seems to be some wandering into the lowlands in the fall: one was reported in the Basin on September 1, 1950; and I found two at Rio Grande Village September 9 through 12, 1969.

Pygmy Nuthatch

Sitta pygmaea

Sporadic winter visitor in the Chisos highlands.

Records range from one fall sighting on November 27, 1981, by C. Sturm, at Boot Spring, to a series of winter and spring sightings from January 28 to April 15, 1967 (Wauer and Russ Wilson). This species nests to the north in the Davis Mountains and about fifty miles to the south in Mexico's Maderas del Carmens.

Creepers:
Family Certhiidae

Brown Creeper

Certhia americana

Sporadic winter visitor and migrant.

Records range from October 20 through May 19. The Brown Creeper was quite common at Rio Grande Village and less numerous in the Chisos woodlands during the 1967–68 winter. I did not see it during the following two winters, but it was present again in the winter of 1970–71, and there were reports in 1975 and 1979 as well. A record of a lone bird searching for insects on a adobe building at Rio Grande Village on August 27, 1975 (Poindyte), is very early.

Wrens:
Family
Troglodytidae

Cactus Wren

Campylorhynchus brunneicapillus

Common resident below the lower edge of the mountain woodlands; rare on the Rio Grande floodplain.

This large desert wren can hardly be missed, because of its loud and raucous call and conspicuous, football-size nests. Nest-building takes place throughout the year, and almost every kind of tree, shrub, and man-made device has been used. Bill Degenhardt reported a nest built in a pair of shorts hanging on the line. My wife discovered a nest in the fold of a sheet one time and in the pocket of my field pants another.

Rock Wren

Salpinctes obsoletus

Uncommon summer resident, common migrant, and fairly common winter resident.

Summertime birds may be found from the cliffs along the river to the top of Emory Peak. Rock Wrens can almost always be found at Hot Springs and on the cliffs at the lower end of the Window Trail. Van Tyne and Sutton (1937) reported a nest with five eggs at Lajitas on May 10, 1935; Henry Howe found it nesting at Grapevine Hills on July 23, 1966; and I found three fledged young on the rocky slope below Laguna Meadow on July 20, 1969.

About the first week of September there is a brief spurt of migrants through the area. Some years this movement increases dramatically from mid-October until early November, when birds are numerous below 5,500 feet. Many apparently remain as winter residents, but winter residents are somewhat sporadic: Chisos Christmas counters recorded 15 in 1966, 14 in 1967, 129 in

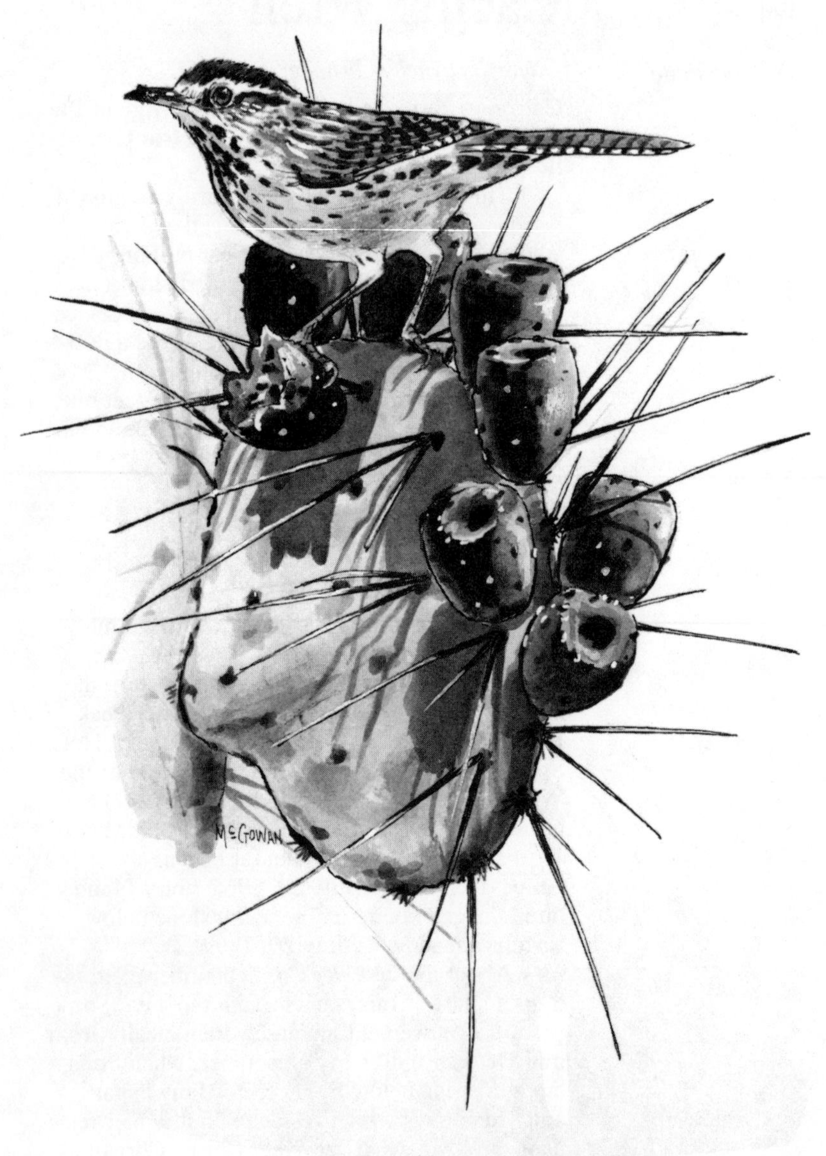

Cactus Wren, *Campylorhynchus brunneicapillus*

1968, 14 in 1969, and 47 in 1970. Another increase in birds is evident in mid-March, and northbound migrants continue to pass through the area until the second week of April.

Canyon Wren

Catherpes mexicanus

Common resident of rocky canyons from the Rio Grande to the top of the Chisos Mountains.

This is the bird with the clear, descending song. You are almost assured of hearing it any sunny morning in Santa Elena Canyon or Boquillas Canyon. Although it prefers rocky cliffs and canyons for nesting and singing, it spends considerable time foraging for food in the mesquite thickets that grow along the river and in lowland washes, or in the piñon-juniper-oak woodlands. Nest-building was found just above the Wilson Ranch in Blue Creek Canyon on April 5, 1969, and adults were seen feeding young at Boquillas on May 24, 1969 (Wauer).

Carolina Wren

Thryothorus ludovicianus

Irregular visitor.

Most sightings are from the river floodplain in the vicinity of Rio Grande Village and Boquillas Crossing, but there also are reports from Panther Junction (David Easterla heard one singing on August 12, 1972), the Chisos Basin (David Simon reported one on August 31, 1967), Laguna Meadow (C. Philip Allen found one there on May 28, 1963), and Boot Spring. There is no evidence of nesting in the park.

Canyon Wren, *Catherpes mexicanus*

Bewick's Wren

Thryomanes bewickii

Abundant summer resident of the Chisos woodlands and less numerous at thickets down to 4,000 feet; fairly common migrant and winter resident.

This is the most numerous summering bird of the park's piñon-juniper-oak woodlands. In fact, its vast repertoire of songs can be very confusing. It can sound very much like a Colima Warbler, and several observations may be necessary before one is sure which song is which. Migrant Bewick's Wrens move through the area from early March to April 9 and from August 27 through October. Migrants and wintering birds can be expected anywhere, but from April 10 to August 27, records are from above 3,500 feet.

House Wren

Troglodytes aedon

Fairly common migrant (April 3–May 12, August 27–early November); uncommon winter resident.

Migrants may be found from the river floodplain to the high Chisos canyons. Some years there appears to be a second fall movement from mid-November to early December. Wintering populations are quite stable and birds can usually be found at Boquillas Crossing, along the Rio Grande Village Nature Trail, near Santa Elena Crossing, and along the Window Trail.

There also are four records of the southern brown-throated form of this wren, which was reclassified as House Wren by the 1983 AOU *Check-list*. I first found one in the Basin on December 3, 1966; T. Paul Bonney reported one at Laguna Meadow on May 19, 1973; Gail Hodge, Georgia Porter, and Rose Marie Stortz found one in the Basin on May 3, 1975; and Chuck Sexton and Becky Lasley reported a well-documented sighting at Rio Grande Village on May 15, 1979. This form is a common nesting wren in the Maderas del Carmen Mountains, fifty miles south of the park.

Winter Wren

Troglodytes troglodytes

Rare migrant (March 2–May 20, November 10–December 27).

Northbound birds can usually be detected by their very distinct song, which they sing over and over again during the early morning. Fall migrants become most numerous November 20 to 24. Except for a sighting at Laguna Meadow on November 15, 1966 (Wauer), and one at the Basin sewage lagoons on May 20, 1978 (Roy Welch), all records of this tiny wren are from the vicinity of the Rio Grande.

Sedge Wren

Cistothorus platensis

Rare winter visitor (December 18–March 8).

I first found one near Boquillas Crossing on February 14, 1967. Mark and Jeanne Leckert reported one at the Gravel Pit on December 13, 1971. Victor Emanuel found one at the Boquillas Canyon Overlook on February 14, 1976; J. R. Bider reported one at Rio Grande Village on March 8, 1977; and Robert Harms reported it at Boquillas on January 2 and 5, 1979. Frances Williams and the Midland Naturalists have recorded it almost every winter below the dam at Lake Balmorhea, where it apparently is a regular winter resident.

Marsh Wren

Cistothorus palustris

Fairly common migrant and winter resident (September 11–May 20) along the Rio Grande.

There is a report of a bird carrying nesting materials at Rio Grande Village on March 27, 1979 (R. Rogers); there is no other evidence of nesting. The bulk of the spring migrants pass through the area from mid-March to early May, but a few stragglers have been reported as late as May 20. During the peak of the northbound movement, the last week of March and the first week of April, this wren is occasionally found a considerable distance from the river; I found one at Oak Creek on March 26 and one at Panther Junction on March 30, 1968.

Fall migrants are not as numerous as those in spring, and the southbound movement is over by mid-November. A high count of fifteen birds was recorded at Rio Grande Village on October 29, 1966 (Wauer). Wintering birds are locally common at such places as the silt pond and the beaver pond at Rio Grande Village.

Kinglets, Gnatcatchers, Thrushes: *Family Muscicapidae*

Golden-crowned Kinglet

Regulus satrapa

Sporadic migrant and winter visitor.

Records range from October 20 to February 25, and there is a late sighting at Boot Spring on March 31, 1968 (Wauer). A few birds can usually be found within the floodplain vegetation below Santa Elena Canyon almost any winter, but the species' occurrence elsewhere is very sporadic. During the winters of 1966–67 and 1967–68, I found it regularly in the high Chisos woodlands; I found a high count of twenty birds along the trail from Boot Spring to the South Rim on January 28, 1967. Except for two individuals in the Basin on October 20, 1969, I have not seen it in the mountains since.

Ruby-crowned Kinglet

Regulus calendula

Abundant migrant and winter resident.

This bird can be the most commonly seen species on the river floodplain and in the higher parts of the mountains from early October through the first week of May. It has been reported as early as August 17 and as late as May 20.

Blue-gray Gnatcatcher

Polioptila caerulea

Common summer resident; fairly common migrant; uncommon and sporadic in winter.

Spring migrants reach the park as early as March 8 (one at Rio Grande Village in 1969), and the northbound movement continues through April 12. Breeding Blue-grays are restricted to the mountain woodlands, and nesting is under way by late March; I found three nests under construction in Boot Canyon on March 30, 1967. Summer birds remain on their breeding grounds until about August 21, when they begin to move out of the area. Northbound birds reach the park at about the same time, and the fall migration continues through October 20. Wintering birds are somewhat sporadic in occurrence; three to five individuals were located on each of the Chisos Mountains Christmas Counts, except in 1969, when none were found.

During migration, when both species of gnatcatchers may be found together in the lowlands, they can be difficult to distinguish. Black-tails do not always have a tail with solid black underparts, and Blue-grays often show considerable darkness in their tail underparts. Their calls are very distinctive, however, and squeaking and hissing will usually arouse them enough to make them call. Black-tail calls are sharper and buzzing; those of Blue-grays are more wheezy or plaintive.

Black-tailed Gnatcatcher

Polioptila melanura

Common resident in the shrub desert below 3,500 feet and rare to 4,000 feet.

Nesting occurs from March through June; Mr. and Mrs. Murl Deusing found a nest with one egg on an allthorn at Dugout Wells on May 17, 1967; I found a nest containing two gnatcatcher eggs and a single Brown-headed Cowbird egg on a mesquite at Nine Point Draw on June 6, 1969. Before nesting, the bird is very vociferous, but it becomes quiet and sometimes difficult to find during nesting. As soon as the young are fledged, one can again easily detect its whereabouts by its constant loud, buzzing call. Although it is considered to be resident, there is an obvious decrease in its numbers during November and an increase in mid-February. A search among the open mesquite flats along the river from Boquillas Canyon to Santa Elena Canyon and along the lower desert washes will always disclose at least a few of these little desert birds.

Eastern Bluebird

Sialia sialis

Uncommon and somewhat sporadic winter resident (November 14–March 24).

There is one nesting record: on April 15, 18, and 23 and May 2, 1972, I observed a lone adult male feeding four spotted youngsters in the vicinity of the lake at Rio Grande Village. The youngsters were barely able to fly on April 15. Dick Youse first found Eastern Bluebirds in the park near Santa Elena Canyon on March 24, 1956. I found them present at Rio Grande Village throughout the winter of 1966–67: three individuals were seen on November 24; more than forty were counted on November 26; and seven individuals were last seen there on March 18. Less than a dozen birds spent the 1967–68 winter at Rio Grande Village from December 21 to March 9, and about two dozen wintered there from December 27, 1968, through March 21, 1969; three were found in the Chisos Basin on December 23. Only ten birds were seen at Rio Grande Village from November 22, 1969, to February 18, 1970, and about two dozen birds wintered there in 1970–71. Pansy Espy has recorded this species from December through March in the Davis Mountains.

Western Bluebird

Sialia mexicana

Rare migrant and fairly common winter visitor.

Records range from October 23 to March 31, and C. Philip Allen reported it at Boot Spring on May 24, 1963. Twenty to thirty birds frequent Boot Canyon and Laguna Meadow to the top of the Emory Peak section of the high Chisos Mountains during mild winter days and move into the lower basins during colder days. These birds spend considerable time soaring

Western Bluebird, *Sialia mexicana*

along the upper ridges and pinnacles. On November 4, 1967, I found a flock of seventeen, twelve of which were seen eating mistletoe berries along the slope above Boot Spring. There are only two lowland records of this species: Harold Brodrick saw a flock at Panther Junction on October 23, 1959, and I found three birds at Rio Grande Village on November 3, 1969. Western Bluebirds nest in the Davis and Maderas del Carmen mountains.

Mountain Bluebird

Sialia currucoides

Rare spring migrant (March 14–May 9); uncommon and somewhat sporadic winter visitor.

Van Tyne and Sutton (1937) reported specimens from Castolon on May 6, 1935, and a male seen at 6,000 feet in Pine Canyon on May 9, 1933; more recently, I saw 20 birds at Rio Grande Village, March 14 through 24, 1970. Most winter records range from November 5 through December, with one sighting in the Chisos Basin on February 2, 1967 (Wauer). I found a high count of 60 to 75 birds on a grassy flat near San Vicente on November 11, 1967. Some winters this species is abundant within the open valleys of the Del Norte and Davis mountains. Bonnie McKinney reported that a large flock of 100 to 150 birds wintered on the large grassy flats of the Agua Fria Ranch, 65 miles south of Alpine, from October 1980 through March 1981.

Townsend's Solitaire

Myadestes townsendi

Fairly common migrant and winter resident in the higher parts of the Chisos Mountains.

The first of the fall migrants reach the area about October 11, and the southbound movement continues until late November. Several birds were found eating berries from Texas madrones along the Emory Peak ridge on November 15, 1966 (Wauer). Winter residents are never numerous but can usually be found at preferred localities—along the lower Window Trail, along the north slope of Emory Peak, and in lower Boot Canyon. Spring migrants pass through the Big Bend from the last of March to mid-April, and there is a second movement from late April to May 15. There is also a June 10, 1956, sighting from the South Rim (National Park Service files).

Veery

Catharus fuscescens

Very rare spring migrant (March 18–May 12).

George Shier first reported one from Rio Grande Village on March 18, 1969, and another from Castolon on March 19. Byron Griffen found one at Boot Canyon on May 3, 1970. And there are three reports from the Old Sam Nail Ranch in May 1980: it was first seen and photographed by Jim Shiflett and C. C. Wiedenfeld on May 9; Richard Derdeyn saw it on May 10; and Linda Snyder reported it there on May 12.

Gray-cheeked Thrush

Catharus minimus

Rare spring migrant (March 19–May 12).

Mrs. Cleve Bachman found one first at Laguna Meadow on May 10, 1967. George Shier reported it twice: in Pine Canyon on March 19, 1969, and at Glenn Spring on April 17, 1970. David Easterla and Dave Snyder found one at Santa Elena Canyon on April 7, 1971. H. Eshbaugh and B. Mack reported one at Boot Spring on May 6, 1977. Richard Prum and Walter Ellison found one at Boot Spring on May 2, 1979. And Linda Snyder reported one at the Old Sam Nail Ranch on May 12, 1980.

Swainson's Thrush

Catharus ustulatus

Uncommon migrant (May 1–25, September 1–October 21); two winter reports.

Winter sightings were made at Laguna Meadow on February 19, 1978, by Ed Kutac; and on the Window Trail on December 8, 1978, by Helen and George Champtax.

Hermit Thrush

Catharus guttatus

Common migrant and fairly common winter resident.

Early fall migrants may reach the Big Bend area by September 8, but the main southward movement does not begin until late September, reaching a peak in the middle of October and decreasing until early November. Late influxes of migrants are not uncommon; many birds were recorded along the river on December 22, 1968, and I counted more than one hundred on January 26, 1969, along the Window Trail, where only a few had been seen a few days earlier. Wintering birds can usually be found along the river and throughout the canyons of the Chisos Mountains. Spring migrants become evident by mid-March; there is a relatively heavy movement through the park that lasts until April 12, when sightings sharply decrease. This low is followed by a second surge of migrants from April 26 to mid-May, and stragglers have been found as late as June 10, 1969 (Wauer). I have heard the Hermit Thrush sing in migration only twice: there were two birds singing at Boquillas during the morning of March 25, 1967, and two or three on the ridge above Boot Spring during the very rainy morning of May 10, 1969.

Wood Thrush

Hylocichla mustelina

Rare spring migrant.

It has been recorded only during 1967 and 1969. In 1967, I found one at Rio Grande Village on April 5, another in upper Green Gulch (5,600 feet) on April 6, and another at Dugout Wells on April 7. In 1969, I found a lone bird at Hot Springs on May 2.

Rufous-backed Robin

Turdus rufopalliatus

One series of sightings.

A lone bird discovered at Rio Grande Village on October 23, 1966, stayed among the dense mesquite and seepwillow near the *Gambusia* pond for eight days before disappearing. Sharon Wauer and I had an excellent look at it the first day, but it became very shy and difficult to find afterward. This was the first sighting of this Mexican species in Texas, but it has since been recorded in a number of places along the border.

American Robin

Turdus migratorius

Uncommon migrant and fairly common winter visitor.

Records range from October 25 to May 21. This is the well-known robin of gardens and woods that can be found in flocks of hundreds. The largest flocks recorded in the park were 15 individuals that wintered in Laguna Meadow in 1966–67, 45 along the Window Trail on December 29, 1970, and 55 there on March 21, 1971 (Wauer). Although huge flocks can often be encountered in the Del Norte and Davis mountains to the north, robins found in the park are usually alone or in small flocks of less than a dozen birds. They may appear anywhere but rarely remain in one place for more than a week or two.

Four or five birds frequent Rio Grande Village and Cottonwood Campground each winter, and a few can usually be found wintering in the lower canyons of the Chisos Mountains. There is no apparent increase in numbers during migration, but one to ten birds may appear at Hot Springs, Panther Junction, the Basin, or elsewhere. There are also two summer records: I saw a lone immature bird near the Basin sewage lagoons on July 19, 1969, and observed another there on August 24, 1970. I found another immature bird at Laguna Meadow on September 4, 1967. All three of these youngsters were alone and very capable of flight; they presumably were late summer wanderers.

Varied Thrush

Ixoreus naevius

One series of sightings.

The records are from upper Juniper Canyon and Boot Canyon during December 1981 and January 1982. A Varied Thrush was first reported by Bryant Pomrenke, who observed one for five minutes in upper Juniper Canyon on December 7. On December 28, Greg and Becky Lasley found what was probably the same bird in Boot Canyon, and did an excellent drawing and description for the record. And Mark Berrier reported it the third time, in Boot Canyon, on January 10.

Aztec Thrush

Ridgwayia pinicola

Extremely rare visitor during July and August.

An immature bird discovered in Boot Canyon on August 21, 1977, by Mimi and David Wolf represents the first for the park as well as for the state of Texas. Deborah DeKeyzer, a member of the Wolf party, photographed the bird, which was later authenticated by Dr. Eugene Eisenmann, an AOU *Check-list* committee member. The bird was again found on August

25, 1977, by Peter Scott and Steve West, who watched it feed on the ground, scratching among the leaves like a towhee, and on berries in a nearby madrone tree. Chuck Sexton found a bird again in lower Boot Canyon on July 31 and August 1, 1982. And Mark Lochward reported a female Aztec Thrush in Boot Canyon on August 7, 1982. There also is a lone sighting of "two or three" individuals on the Lost Mine Trail by Ed Pace, August 14, 1983.

Mockingbirds, Thrashers: *Family Mimidae*

Gray Catbird

Dumetella carolinensis

Rare spring migrant; rare vagrant anytime.

A series of sightings from March 1963 at Rio Grande Village was all that existed for the park before 1970. Since then it has been reported on a number of occasions throughout the year. Most sightings are from Rio Grande Village, although it has also been seen at the Old Sam Nail Ranch (on May 12, 1978, by David and Mimi Wolf) and in the Chisos Basin (on May 18, 1978, by Andrew Stewart and Ed Kutac, and on June 15, 1982, by Wayne Gordon).

Northern Mockingbird

Mimus polyglottos

Common summer resident and migrant; fairly common winter resident below 5,000 feet.

Summertime birds frequent almost every wash and patch of vegetation from the floodplain to the lower edge of the Chisos woodlands. Nesting has been recorded from April through August, and the breeding birds are considerably

Northern Mockingbird, *Mimus polyglottos*

darker than those in winter. A population decline begins in mid-August and continues through the fall and winter; a low is reached from February 22 to mid-March, when the wintering birds move out of the area. From March 15 to March 17, however, there is a drastic increase in the population as spring migrants begin to pour into the desert lowlands. This high remains until mid-June, when the first of the nesting birds begin to disperse. Some of Big Bend's mockers are permanent residents; a bird banded at Rio Grande Village was recorded there all twelve months of the year. Breeding birds at Panther Junction do not remain in the area, although they return each March and stay until at least mid-July.

Sage Thrasher

Oreoscoptes montanus

Uncommon spring migrant; sporadic in fall and winter.

Records range from September 14 through April 29, and there is one summer sighting of a lone bird along the Window Trail on July 24, 1964, by Dick Rasp, which raises the question of nesting but more likely represents an injured or nonbreeding vagrant. Spring migrants are most common from March 9 to April 7, and I found lone birds at Persimmon Gap on April 21, 1970, and at Hot Springs on April 27, 1968. Fall sightings are infrequent during October, increase during early November, and usually decrease by late November. I found fifteen to twenty individuals near the Adams Ranch, just northeast of the park, on October 13, 1969, and fifty or more birds on Dog Canyon Flat on December 16, 1970. It appears that Sage Thrashers move through the area in numbers, and if such food as the tasajillo cactus fruit is available, they may remain for several days. I have seen several birds on the flat just west of the Boquillas Canyon parking area almost every year during the first two weeks of November.

Brown Thrasher

Toxostoma rufum

Uncommon migrant and winter resident.

The Brown Thrasher has been recorded from September 26 through May 20. Most sightings are from the floodplain at Rio Grande Village, the Santa Elena Canyon picnic area, and Cottonwood Campground, but I also have found it regularly in winter at the Old Sam Nail Ranch. Lone birds are usual, but migrants may be seen in twos and threes.

Long-billed Thrasher

Toxostoma longirostre

Rare migrant.

The status of this species has changed in recent years; it was recorded in the park only twice before 1970, but twelve times from 1976 through 1983. The majority of reports occur from March 10 through June 6, and there are two summer reports from the Old Sam Nail Ranch: Richard Schaefer found one there on July 2, 1982, and M. Parker and F. Freese observed two there on August 2, 1983. Bonnie McKinney captured, banded, and photographed a bird at Black Gap Wildlife Management Area, just north of the park, on June 4, 1983. This bird is common in the Southeast Texas brushland as far west as Del Rio; increased records in the Big Bend Country may relate to the clearing of brushland in Southeast Texas and adjacent Mexico.

Bendire's Thrasher

Toxostoma bendirei

Rare vagrant almost anywhere below the mountain woodlands.

This western thrasher appears to have extended its range eastward into the Big Bend Country recently. It was first reported by Laurie Yorke, who watched one "singing occasionally" at Dugout Wells on August 27, 1977. It was next reported on December 26, 1978, when R. J. Bullock, Mary Louise Stewart, and Bruce Stewart found one at Hot Springs. In 1980, Nancy and Jerry Strickling found one at Dugout Wells on January 8, and Bruce Stewart reported one from Boquillas on December 26. None were reported in 1981 and 1982, but there are three 1983 reports: Jeanne Pratt found one on Dagger Flat, January 30; Brete Griffin, Ann Tews, and Mark Kirtley reported one at the Panther Junction trailer area on February 27; and Gerry and Vicki Wolfe reported one at the Chisos Basin lagoons on August 21. Bonnie McKinney reported one at Black Gap Wildlife Management Area on July 19, 1982.

Curve-billed Thrasher

Toxostoma curvirostre

Rare in summer, common migrant, and fairly common winter resident below 5,000 feet.

This is a species that may have decreased as a breeding bird within the park during recent years. Van Tyne and Sutton reported it to nest at Glenn Spring in May 1932, and Harold Brodrick found it nesting at Panther Junction in 1961. More recently, I have found it to summer only along the northern edge of the park in the vicinity of Paint Gap, and in 1971 it nested at Panther Junction; a juvenile bird, barely able to fly, was banded there on June 6. I had seen adults throughout May for the first time in five years. Curve-billed Thrashers are fairly common on the open mesquite lands of northern Brewster County and north to Fort Stockton and Fort Davis.

Curve-billed Thrasher, *Toxostoma curvirostre*

Fall migrants reach the park area by late August; an immature bird, probably a wanderer and not a local youngster, was seen along the Window Trail on August 27, 1968. This bird can be found almost anywhere in the lowlands from late October through May, and it arrives at Panther Junction on October 15 and remains until April 19. It is most numerous as a migrant from mid-March to May 16, and a few stragglers are recorded to June 14. Singing birds have been recorded in migration and on their wintering grounds. The earliest song I recorded was at Panther Junction on February 11, 1969. Although most migrants pass through the lowlands, there are several Basin sightings and one from Laguna Meadow on December 23, 1967 (Wauer).

Crissal Thrasher

Toxostoma dorsale

Uncommon summer and winter resident and migrant.

This species may be filling the niche vacated by the decreasing Curve-billed Thrasher. Crissal Thrashers nest in a rather wide zone of habitats from the acacia-mesquite-arroyo association to the Chisos chaparral, from 3,500 to 6,500 feet. Van Tyne and Sutton (1937) reported it as a nesting bird at 5,200 feet in the Basin only, but recent nesting records range from Laguna Meadow, Blue Creek Canyon, and along the Window Trail to Dugout Wells and the K-Bar Ranch—all during May and June. Mike Parmeter and I found nest-building in Blue Creek Canyon on May 8, 1969; Ty and Julie Hotchkiss discovered a nest in a mesquite at the K-Bar the first week of May 1970; and I observed an adult feeding three youngsters along the Window Trail on May 25, 1969.

Postnesting birds wander into the lowlands and may be found along the river at Rio Grande Village and Castolon during the summer. The Crissal Thrasher is most numerous as a migrant

Crissal Thrasher, *Toxostoma dorsale*

from mid-March to April 10 and August 22 to early November. Wintering birds can usually be found among the dense mesquite thickets along the river and up into the Chisos chaparral zones. A search near Cottonwood Campground, the flats just north of the Santa Elena Canyon picnic area, and along the Window Trail just below the sewage lagoons can usually produce at least a few Crissal Thrashers.

Pipits:
Family Motacillidae

Water Pipit

Anthus spinoletta

Fairly common migrant and winter visitor.

Fall migrants may arrive as early as September 24 but are more common from mid-October to late November. Spring migrants are most numerous from mid-March through May 11, and stragglers continue to pass through the area until May 28. Most records are from the river and creeks, but this bird may be found in the mountains as well; there are several sightings from the Basin, and I found lone birds at Boot Spring on May 8, 1968, and at Laguna Meadow on May 10, 1969. Flocks of 8 to 20 birds are common, but a flock of 75 was seen along the River Road near San Vicente on November 11, 1967 (Wauer). Wintering birds are almost totally confined to the river and adjacent grassy flats, although they occasionally visit upper Tornillo and Terlingua creeks.

Sprague's Pipit

Anthus spragueii

Rare migrant (March 20–May 6, October 8–December 16).

There is also one record of two individuals at Banta Shut-in on February 10 and 11, 1979 (Steve Zachary). This buff-colored ground dweller prefers grassy fields and stays away from open places more than the preceding species. A walk through grassy flats in late October may flush out one or more of these very shy birds. When frightened, Water Pipits will usually fly some distance in a flock before alighting and walking about. The Sprague's Pipit will suddenly fly out—almost at your feet—from the protection of a clump of grass, fly up into the air (usually alone rather than with a flock), and then alight and hide among the grass clumps. Its characteristic flight and distinctive call note readily separate this species from the more common Water Pipit.

Waxwings: *Family Bombycillidae*

Cedar Waxwing

Bombycilla cedrorum

Uncommon migrant and winter visitor, but sporadic along the river in spring.

There are only a few fall sightings: I found it at Panther Junction on October 12, 1970, and October 29, 1957, and at Laguna Meadow on November 4, 1967; Doug Evans saw it at Boot Spring on November 15, 1963. From late November until mid-March, it is an occasional visitor along the river, at lowland springs, and in the lower mountains. A small flock of 10 to 25 birds may remain at a particularly good feeding area for a few hours to a few days and then move on. Some years, during the last half of March, Cedar Waxwings become numerous along the river, and flocks of a dozen to 200 birds can be found. A flock of 180 to 200 was seen daily at Rio Grande Village from April 25 to May 19, 1969. A few remained there until May 27.

Silky Flycatchers: *Family Ptilogonatidae*

Phainopepla

Phainopepla nitens

Rare in summer; uncommon migrant and winter resident.

The status of this species is uncertain. Apparently, it does nest within the area some years; Pete Koch found a nest in lower Green Gulch in 1947, and I found a pair of birds courting in Big Brushy Canyon, south of Black Gap Wildlife Management Area, on May 22, 1970. Lone birds or small groups sighted in June and early July—such as a male and two females I saw flying south over the Rio Grande Village area on

July 3, 1970—are probably postnesting individuals.

Southbound migrants occur in small flocks along the river and in lower canyons of the Chisos during September and October. By November this species seems to remain at localized areas for longer periods of time; for example, I saw two birds near Nine Point Draw four times from November 10 to 21, 1967. Wintering birds are irregular in occurrence but have been reported most often from lower Green Gulch and just west of the Basin Campground. There is a slight increase in numbers in early March, and this apparent northbound movement continues through mid-April; Charles Crabtree reported "several" individuals along the Dodson Trail and on Mesa de Anguila, April 7 to 10, 1971. This increase is followed by another lapse of records and another increase in sightings from late April to May 28.

Shrikes:
Family Laniidae

Loggerhead Shrike

Lanius ludovicianus

Uncommon summer resident; common migrant and winter resident.

Nesting occurs during April, May, and June within the sotol grasslands and yucca zones of the park. A nest found May 28, 1968, on a Torrey yucca at 3,000 feet near Dugout Wells contained four eggs (Wauer). This bird is very shy during the nesting season and is rarely seen then, but it is more easily found after late July, when postnesting visitors and early fall migrants begin to move into the lowlands. This high population decreases somewhat by November, but wintering birds remain common below 4,500 feet. Felix Hernandez III reported watching a Loggerhead Shrike attempting to kill a House Sparrow, which escaped, at Panther Junction on February 9, 1980.

Starlings:
Family Sturnidae

European Starling

Sturnus vulgaris

Rare vagrant within the park; more common at settled areas north of the park.

The first park record was of a lone bird seen at Rio Grande Village in January 1965 (Mr. and Mrs. C. Edgar Bedell). I found one there with several Brewer's Blackbirds on April 28, 1967, and observed three starlings on both October 31 and December 10. I saw lone birds at Rio Grande Village on May 6 and 8, 1968, and at Cottonwood Campground on December 22, 1969. Bert Hensel reported it at Rio Grande Village on November 28, 1979. It can be expected to increase at developed areas of the Big Bend but will likely remain merely a vagrant in Big Bend National Park because of the park's wilderness character.

Vireos:
Family Vireonidae

White-eyed Vireo

Vireo griseus

Rare spring migrant (February 16–April 27); one late fall record.

Johnny Armstrong reported one at Rio Grande Village on November 26, 1982. Except for a single report near Cattail Falls, on April 18, 1983, by Bruce Talbot, all other records are from the vicinity of the Rio Grande.

Bell's Vireo

Vireo bellii

Abundant summer resident (March 8–September 29) along the Rio Grande floodplain.

It also occurs in smaller numbers at other suitable places, such as Dugout Wells, the Old Sam Nail Ranch, Oak Creek, and similar thickets up to 4,500 feet. Early spring arrivals and late fall birds are quiet except for very early morning singing. By March 24 their song is one of the most commonly heard along the floodplain. Nesting occurs from April through June: I found a fledged bird at Rio Grande Village on May 10, 1968, a nest with young at Oak Creek on May 14, 1967, and an active nest located twelve feet high in a cottonwood at Castolon on June 7, 1969. Most of the summering birds move out of the area by the second week of September, but an occasional individual can usually be found for another couple of weeks.

Black-capped Vireo

Vireo atricapillus

Summer resident (April 19–August 19) at localized areas only.

This little vireo was reported within the park only three times before 1966: Dick Youse found one in upper Blue Creek Canyon on May 20, 1956; Jerry Strickling saw two at Kibby Spring on May 13, 1962; and Ben and Joan Trimble and Malcolm Jenkins reported two along the Window Trail on August 15, 1963. On May 5, 1966, Jon Barlow found it nesting in Campground Canyon on the south slope of Pulliam Ridge. Since then it has been seen in this and adjacent canyons every year. I found a nest with three eggs there on May 18, 1967; David Easterla found one male feeding young out of the nest on July 5, 1967; David Wolf and Nicholas Halmi reported two immature birds there on August 19, 1977. It has also been reported, at lesser intervals, on the north side of Pulliam Ridge (Jim Liles) and at Panther Canyon, Green Gulch, Blue Creek Canyon, and Juniper Canyon. There appears to be some postnesting wandering; I found a juvenile within a heavily wooded area below Emory Peak at 6,100 feet on August 7, 1969; and David Wolf reported one female and one immature at Rio Grande Village on September 7, 1973.

Gray Vireo

Vireo vicinior

Fairly common summer resident at suitable localities; rare migrant and winter resident.

Males arrive on their breeding grounds as early as March 17 and can easily be detected by their distinct three-whistle song. Males vigorously defend their territories throughout the breeding period and are one of the park's most vociferous species at that time. Six singing birds were found in Blue Creek Canyon on May 8, 1969; from about one mile above the ranch house, territorial birds were found approximately every quarter-mile (Wauer). A more accessible breeding habitat lies directly across Oak Creek Canyon from the Basin Campground. Most of the canyons along the south slope of Pulliam Ridge contain one or two breeding pairs of Gray Vireos from late April through early June. Jon Barlow studied the Gray Vireo in these canyons during the summers of 1966 and 1967.

There is some postnesting dispersal; I found lone birds at Panther Junction on June 18, 1967; on the Lost Mine Trail on July 23, 1967; and in Panther Canyon on August 23, 1970. Patty Easterla found one at Panther Junction on June 6, 1971. Records of migrants are scarce; I found singing males in the center of Boquillas Canyon on March 22, 1968, and at Dugout Wells on October 8, 1968. Winter sightings are few, too: Karl Haller first reported one in the Chisos Basin on December 24, 1950, and Jon Barlow and I recorded it near the Chimneys and at Robber's Roost on December 30, 1970, and January 3, 1971 (Barlow and Wauer, 1971). Since then it has been reported frequently in winter for the lower brushy washes below 3,500 feet.

Gray Vireo, *Vireo vicinior*

Solitary Vireo

Vireo solitarius

Rare in summer and winter; fairly common migrant.

It appears that this species nests in Boot Canyon only during wet years. A pair was found courting at Boot Spring on May 12, 1968; none were seen in the summer of 1969, but I found a male defending a territory at Boot Spring on May 7, 8, and 9, 1970. The spring of 1971 was very dry, and I did not find this bird in Boot Canyon; however, I did find a pair in upper Campground Canyon on June 16. Jon Barlow found it to be a fairly common nesting bird in Madera Canyon in the Davis Mountains during May and June 1968.

It is most numerous as a migrant; as such it can be found from the river floodplain to the highest parts of the Chisos Mountains. It may appear as early as February 24; Van Tyne and Sutton (1937) reported one in Green Gulch in 1935. In recent years I have recorded it regularly after March 11; a peak is reached April 1 through 11, when the majority of the birds are of the small, yellow-green *cassinii* race. There is a paucity of sightings from April 12 to 21, followed by another heavy movement that lasts until May 17, peaking between May 2 and 9. The majority of these latter birds are the larger and lighter *plumbeous* race.

Fall migrants may reach the park area as early as August 15 but are most numerous September 8 through 25; stragglers continue to pass through the area until mid-December. I found lone birds at Laguna Meadow on November 5, 1968, in the Basin on November 24, 1968, and on the Lost Mine Trail on December 16, 1966. The majority of the fall migrants are large and light, but an occasional yellow-green bird is found. There is also a handful of winter sightings from Rio Grande Village and Cottonwood Campground.

Yellow-throated Vireo

Vireo flavifrons

Four park records.

Jon Barlow saw one first, just above the cottages in the Chisos Basin on May 13, 1967; I observed one foraging among the pines with several Townsend's and Orange-crowned Warblers in upper Boot Canyon, September 29, 1969; Stuart Tingley reported one for Rio Grande Village on April 7, 1978; and Jim Shiflett and C. C. Wiedenfeld found a singing bird at Cottonwood Campground on May 9, 1980.

Hutton's Vireo, *Vireo huttoni*

Hutton's Vireo

Vireo huttoni

Fairly common summer resident and uncommon winter resident within the Chisos woodlands.

Nesting takes place during April, May, and June; a nest was found in a clump of mistletoe on an oak at Laguna Meadow on April 29, 1935 (Van Tyne and Sutton, 1937), nest-building was found there on May 17, 1969, and an adult was seen feeding a fledged bird at Boot Spring on June 9, 1968 (Wauer). Nesting birds are generally restricted to the upper parts of the woodlands, above 5,800 feet. I counted eleven singing birds between the upper Basin and Laguna Meadow on March 30, 1968. Its loud *sweeet* call can be heard for more than a hundred feet, and a few loud squeaks or hisses in the proper habitat can usually attract one or two birds. Soon after nesting, it moves into lower canyons, where it may remain throughout the winter; it can often be found in oak groves, such as those along the lower end of the Window Trail and near the east side of Panther Pass. Hutton's Vireos may wander below the woodlands on occasion; I found two individuals about three hundred feet below the piñon-junipers in Blue Creek Canyon on February 1, 1969.

Warbling Vireo

Vireo gilvus

Rare in summer and uncommon in migration.

The summering status of this vireo in the mountains is similar to that of the Solitary Vireo; it nests in the high Chisos canyons during the wet years only. I saw a pair of Warbling Vireos at Boot Spring on May 3 and 14 and June 11, 1967, and found a nest among the foliage of a Grave's oak at Boot Spring on June 8, 1968. And there are three nesting records for the riparian areas at Rio Grande Village and Cottonwood Campground: Harold Holt found nests at both sites on May 12, 1976, and Wayne Gordon reported a nest at Cottonwood Campground on June 15, 1982. It is most numerous in migration from mid-April to late May, when it can be found along the river or at oak groves in the mountains. Fall migrants are not as numerous, and sightings range from early August to early November, mainly in the lowlands.

Philadelphia Vireo

Vireo philadelphicus

Rare migrant (April 8–May 7, August 7–October 24).

Except for one report by Jim Liles at Panther Junction on April 30 and May 1, 1980, all sightings are from the vicinity of the Rio Grande.

Red-eyed Vireo

Vireo olivaceus

Rare spring migrant (April 19–May 20) in the lowlands.

There is a single late summer sighting by Steve West at Boquillas on August 12, 1978. There is also a lone report for the Chisos Basin, by Jimmy Homer, on June 21, 1976. Two park records exist for the Yellow-green Vireo, now considered a race only (AOU, 1983); David Easterla collected a singing male at Cottonwood Campground on July 13, 1972, and Mark Tuttle reported a singing bird at Rio Grande Village on May 7 and 8, 1980.

Wood Warblers: *Family Emberizidae, Subfamily Parulinae*

Blue-winged Warbler

Vermivora pinus

Four records for the park.

Three of the sightings are from the Rio Grande Village Nature Trail: Adele Harding first saw one there on April 28, 1966; I found one there on May 11, 1970; and Bert and Millie Schaughency saw one on August 24, 1971. On

May 7, 1983, Bonnie McKinney and Nancy Flood found one at Boot Spring.

Golden-winged Warbler

Vermivora chrysoptera

Two records for the park.

Charles Crabtree and I found one among the oaks in Boot Canyon on May 9, 1970, and Peter Scott observed a male at Rio Grande Village on May 3, 1978.

Tennessee Warbler

Vermivora peregrina

Two sightings in the park.

Bruce Stewart first reported one he observed many times from December 20 through 23, 1978, at Rio Grande Village; and Will Risser reported one at Rio Grande Village on May 3, 1980.

Orange-crowned Warbler

Vermivora celata

Fairly common migrant and winter resident.

Spring migrants begin to move through the Big Bend Country the second week of March, reach a peak from March 24 to April 11, and gradually decrease in numbers until May 13. Southbound migrants have been recorded as early as August 12, and a peak is reached from October 18 to November 5. There are a few instances when small flocks were recorded; for example, I found eight birds at Rio Grande Village on September 5, 1969. Wintering Orange-crowns are fairly common until early January, when there is a noticeable decrease in numbers. This population low continues until the first of the spring migrants put in their appearance.

Nashville Warbler

Vermivora ruficapilla

Fairly common migrant (March 23–May 15, August 24–October 24).

This is one of the earliest of the spring warblers and is a good indicator that the spring migration has started. Although it is never abundant, small flocks of three to ten birds can often be found at all elevations throughout the period of migration. There also is a series of sightings at Rio Grande Village, November 18 through 25, 1973, by Albertine Bauguess.

Virginia's Warbler

Vermivora virginiae

Uncommon migrant in spring (April 14–May 24) and rare in fall.

Most sightings are from the mountains, but it has also been recorded along the river. At Rio Grande Village I found one on May 1, 1969, two on May 20, 1967, and one on May 24, 1967; at the Santa Elena Canyon picnic area, I found one on May 1, 1967. Fall sightings include six birds found in the oaks at 4,400 feet in Panther Canyon on August 23, 1970; one at Rio Grande Village on September 6, 1968; and two at Cottonwood Campground on September 15, 1969 (Wauer). Highland birds may be confused with the more numerous Colima Warbler.

Colima Warbler

Vermivora crissalis

Common resident in Boot Canyon and less numerous at a few other localities in the upper canyons of the Chisos Mountains.

This is probably Big Bend's most famous bird. It is found nowhere else in the United States, and it winters in relatively inaccessible mountainous areas in southwestern Mexico. It has been recorded in the Chisos Mountains as early as March 15 but usually does not arrive until the first or second week of April.

During April, May, and June, there is no problem finding Colimas at the proper habitat. They are vociferous; males sing throughout the day prior to nesting but only in the early morning and on a few occasions during the day while nesting. Nests are located on the ground in leaf litter or under clumps of grass. Both adults build the nest, incubate the eggs, and care for the young. I have banded nestlings ready to leave the nest from May 25 to July 6. Very little attention is given the young after they have been out of the nest a few days.

By late June the Colima may be more difficult to find. Searching among the oaks in the proper localities, however, will usually turn up at least a few individuals. If a birder enters an oak grove and remains for several minutes, he or she will often find Colimas beginning to move about among the heavier foliage of the oaks and adjacent broadleaf trees and shrubs.

Postnesting birds remain on their breeding grounds until mid-July, when there is a noticeable decrease in Colimas. However, they can usually be found in Boot Canyon throughout August and early September; the latest sighting is September 19. The best place in the park to find this bird is along the trail in Boot Canyon just above the cabin at Boot Spring.

Colima Warbler, *Vermivora crissalis*

The Colima also occurs at a number of other localities within the Chisos Mountains. Annual counts were taken during the second week of May in 1967 through 1970. All locations where suitable habitats exist were searched. Totals of 92 Colima Warblers were found in 1967, 130 in 1968, 166 in 1969, 118 in 1970. In all instances it was associated with oak-piñon-juniper or oak–maple–Arizona cypress environments. Approximately 85 percent of the birds counted were located along a narrow and relatively humid canyon with considerable overstory of vegetation, and 15 percent were found on relatively open slopes and ridges. Some localities appear to offer quite stable habitats, whereas others vary considerably. All the Boot Canyon drainages were heavily used every year, but considerable variation of populations occurs in fringe areas like Laguna Meadow and its canyons, Emory Peak, and upper Pine Canyon. In general, the distribution of breeding birds appears to be determined by the precipitation during the months just before the nesting season. During wet spring months, as in 1968, Colimas were found nesting along the trail just below Laguna Meadow and in upper Pine Canyon. During dry years, such as 1969, more were found in the higher canyons and fewer in such lower and drier canyons as Pine Canyon and below Laguna Meadow.

Lucy's Warbler

Vermivora luciae

Extremely rare migrant.

Noberto Ortega and I saw a singing male among the mesquites at Rio Grande Village on April 8, 1970. I collected a singing male at Boquillas on April 17 and found two more individuals at Rio Grande Village on May 3, 1970. In spite of searching this same area for several days afterward, I was unable to find it again. In 1972, I found lone singing birds at Rio Grande Village on April 4 and 23. Since this habitat seems to be identical to that used by nesting birds in Arizona and New Mexico, it may become established sometime in the future, if it does not already nest in some out-of-the-way mesquite thickets along the floodplain. Steve West informed me that this bird has nested near El Paso. And Tony Gallucci found it nesting near Candelaria in April and May 1978; four fledglings were seen on May 20.

Northern Parula

Parula americana

Rare in summer, winter, and fall; uncommon spring migrant.

It appears that this little warbler has increased in numbers in recent years. There were no park records before 1967, but it has been seen regularly since then. All of the records are from the lowlands, except for a few in spring during migration: at the Old Sam Nail Ranch on April 15, 1967 (Ruth Black and Barbara Ribble); at Dugout Wells on April 29, 1971 (Carl Prytherch and William Smith); and on the Window Trail on April 18, 1976 (John and Barbara Ribble).

Yellow Warbler

Dendroica petechia

Fairly common migrant (April 15–June 18, August 11–September 15); formerly a common nesting species along the Rio Grande.

Van Tyne and Sutton (1937) reported that it nested in Boquillas, Hot Springs, and San Vicente during the 1930s, but I have searched the floodplain for nesting birds without success. In five years (1966–71) I found only three summertime birds: lone males at Rio Grande Village on June 18, 1967, and July 30, 1970, and at Boquillas Crossing on July 15, 1967. Phillips, Marshall, and Monson (1964) believe that nesting Yellow Warblers have been extirpated by parasitism of Brown-headed Cowbirds in some parts of southern Arizona, and this may well be the case in the Big Bend; cowbirds have increased in recent years and are now abundant along the river floodplain where Yellow Warblers once nested.

Migrants have been seen yearly. At Rio Grande Village in 1970, five spring migrants were found on April 26, fifteen on May 4, more than twenty on May 17, and none on May 19. Fall migrants are less numerous than spring migrants.

Chestnut-sided Warbler

Dendroica pensylvanica

Four records for the park.

Specimens were taken at Rio Grande Village on May 13 (one of two birds seen) and October 5, 1969 (Wauer). I observed one there on October 10, 1970. Gary Berg reported one at the Old Sam Nail Ranch on June 2, 1980.

Magnolia Warbler

Dendroica magnolia

Four spring records (April 20–May 18); three fall records.

Two of the spring records are for Rio Grande Village, but two are for the Old Sam Nail Ranch: I observed a lone male foraging among the leaves of a walnut tree there on May 18, 1969, and Jim Shiflett reported one on May 9, 1980. J. R. Barnwell made two fall sightings at Rio Grande Village on October 10, 1972, and Stoney Burdick and I observed one there on October 29, 1971.

Cape May Warbler

Dendroica tigrina

Extremely rare migrant.

Until 1976, this bird was considered only hypothetical for the park, on the basis of one report by Charles T. Meyer and Michael D.

Stuart for Government Spring on May 19, 1969. In 1976, there were nine reports of a lone male at the Old Sam Nail Ranch and one report from Rio Grande Village, all between April 18 and May 2, by (in order of reporting) Barbara Ribble, John Pond, Mr. and Mrs. Glenn Smith, Jean Bensmiller, Donald Billiard, Paul Krapfel, Larry Pearler, Kevin Zimmer, Scott Robinson, Robert Anderson, Charles Gill, Bill Smith, Skip Nichols, David McCorquodale and Sid Andrews (at Rio Grande Village), and Mary Ann Payne. There is one additional report: L. deMarch observed one at Rio Grande Village on May 24, 1979.

Black-throated Blue Warbler

Dendroica caerulescens

Rare spring migrant (May 5–June 22); accidental in late fall and winter.

On June 22, 1971, Patty Easterla found a dead female below the window of a house at Panther Junction; the previous night had been very stormy. Among other records, Anne Bellamy found one at Panther Junction on November 3, 1981; Albertine and Walter Bauguess reported one male with a wave of warblers at Rio Grande Village on November 18, 1973; Robert Harms found one at Rio Grande Village on January 3, 1979; Jody Miller observed one there on February 12, 1975; and Jack and Phyllis Wilburn reported a female at the Old Sam Nail Ranch on March 30, 1979.

Yellow-rumped Warbler

Dendroica coronata

Both forms of the Yellow-rumped Warbler occur

within the Big Bend Country. Recent studies by Hubbard (1969) indicate that they are one species, but they are treated as two species here because they can be separated by field characteristics. Typical male Audubon's have yellow throats and a large, white wing patch, whereas typical male Myrtle Warblers have white throats and two distinct white wing bars. This coloration is rather vague in winter birds and females, but there is another good method of separating these two birds: the rear of the black cheek patch turns up in the Myrtle but joins the dark on the chest or throat in the Audubon's.

Myrtle Warbler

Fairly common migrant in spring and rare in fall; uncommon winter resident.

Park records range in date from October 18 through May 13. October and November birds are few and far between, but there is a slight increase in December. Wintering birds usually can be found along the river with the more common Audubon's Warbler. There are but two winter records elsewhere: Dick Youse found one at the Old Sam Nail Ranch on February 12, 1965, and I saw one in the Basin on December 22, 1967. Myrtle Warblers begin to increase slightly in numbers toward the last of February and by mid-March are as numerous in the lowlands as Audubon's Warblers. A peak is reached in early April, but stragglers continue to pass through the park until mid-May.

Audubon's Warbler

Common migrant and winter resident.

Records range from September 5 to May 27. Except for about two weeks during the first part of April, this is the common bird of the "Myrtebon" complex. This western warbler is most numerous as a spring migrant from late March through mid-May. There are several late May records as well, and D. R. Love saw one at Boquillas on June 5, 1962. C. Philip Allen reported seeing 40 birds at Boot Spring on April 27, 1963, and I counted 58 along the canyon on May 12, 1967; only one was seen at Rio Grande Village on May 24, 1967.

Fall migrants do not seem to be as numerous throughout the park as spring migrants, but larger flocks or "waves" have been recorded in fall. On August 30, 1966, I found 150 or more individuals with several Ruby-crowned Kinglets, Townsend's Warblers, and White-breasted Nuthatches at Laguna Meadow. On September 25, 1966, I recorded a "wave of birds near the East Rim at 8:30 a.m., including 35 to 40 Audubon's Warblers, and many Townsend's Warblers with a few Hermit Thrushes, Hepatic Tanagers, Ruby-crowned Kinglets, and Vesper Sparrows." Early fall sightings are all in the mountains, and the earliest sighting along the river is of three birds on September 5, 1969 (Wauer). The fall movement subsides by early November, but birds remain common along the river and uncommon above 4,500 feet for the first half of the winter, or until the first good series of northers reaches the Big Bend. Afterward it is almost impossible to find this bird in the mountains until the first of the spring migrants begin to move into the area in late March.

Black-throated Gray Warbler

Dendroica nigrescens

Rare spring migrant (March 30–April 27); uncommon fall migrant (August 3–October 4, rare after September 9); a few winter sightings (January 1–February 11).

Dingus and Mr. and Mrs. C. Edgar Bedell reported one at Rio Grande Village throughout January 1965, and Peter and Ruth Isleib found it there on February 3. Tom Will reported four in the Chisos Basin on January 4, 1975; Stephen and Janet Hinshaw observed one male along the Window Trail on January 27, 1974; and Keith and Jan Wiggers reported one at Rio Grande Village on February 11, 1979.

Townsend's Warbler

Dendroica townsendi

Fairly common migrant and sporadic winter resident.

Spring migrants move through the park area from early April though May 12. A peak is reached from May 1 to 10, when the Townsend's can be found in numbers at all elevations, although it is most numerous in the mountain woodlands. On May 8, 1967, I heard several singing on the hillside above Boot Spring, but I could not find a single bird the following morning.

Fall migrants reach the park as early as August 8 but do not become numerous until the end of the month and on through mid-September; stragglers continue to pass through the area until mid-November. The high fall count was 28 individuals found along the trail between the Basin Trailhead and the South Rim on September 4, 1966 (Wauer).

Wintering birds occur sporadically. I have found this species regularly from December through February every year except 1969–70. Most wintertime sightings are from Laguna Meadow and near Boot Spring.

Hermit Warbler

Dendroica occidentalis

Uncommon migrant (April 21–May 14, August 5–September 28).

A specimen taken in the Basin on May 3, 1935 (Van Tyne and Sutton, 1937), was the first for Texas. The Hermit Warbler has since been reported a number of times. It was seen near Laguna Meadow by Robert C. Stein on May 4, 1961; Anne LeSassier found it at Boot Spring on

Townsend's Warbler, *Dendroica townsendi*

April 26, 1972, on April 28, 1967, and May 9, 1968. Fall records include a specimen found in upper Boot Canyon on August 8, 1969, and lone birds at Rio Grande Village on August 28, 1969, at Boot Spring on September 28, 1969, and August 29, 1970, at Laguna Meadow on August 30, 1970, and in the Basin on August 31, 1966 (Wauer). Pansy Espy has recorded it in the Davis Mountains on four occasions from August 5 to 31.

Black-throated Green Warbler

Dendroica virens

Rare spring migrant; one fall record.

The fall record is a bird I collected in upper Boot Canyon on August 8, 1969. Springtime records range from March 21 (a lone male reported at Dugout Wells by Ron Spomer in 1980) to May 12 (I observed one with three Audubon's Warblers at the South Rim at dusk in 1967). It appears that the majority of sightings fall during the brief period of May 9 to 12.

Golden-cheeked Warbler

Dendroica chrysoparia

Four reports for the park.

F. R. Gehlbach and his students reported it first: a singing male in upper Boot Canyon on April 9, 1968. Next, Chris Seifert and Carol Brubaker reported a lone male at Cattail Falls on April 7, 1978. H. P. Langridge found one male in Boot Canyon on July 10, 1978, and Tyrrel Harvey, Steve Hawkins, and Richard Schaefer reported one at Boot Spring on July 12, 1980.

Blackburnian Warbler

Dendroica fusca

Five park records (May 6–22).

Doyle and Helen Peckham and I watched an adult male foraging for insects among the foliage at the beaver pond on the Rio Grande Village Nature Trail, May 6, 1970. It was next seen at Rio Grande Village on May 22, 1978, and reported separately by Dennis Luton and Dean Fisher. There were three separate sightings in 1983: at Rio Grande Village on May 9 (Mabel Bendixen and Kristin Larson); at Sotol Vista on May 10 (Mabel Bendixen); and on the Pinnacles in the upper Chisos Basin on May 11 (Bob Honig and Tommy Michael).

Yellow-throated Warbler

Dendroica dominica

Rare spring migrant (March 7–April 29).
The majority of sightings are from Rio Grande Village, but two are from Panther Junction: Robert DeVine reported one there on March 7 and 8, 1980, and Jim Liles found one male there on April 9, 1983.

Grace's Warbler

Dendroica graciae

Rare migrant (April 18–June 1, August 8–September 24).
All but three of the records are from the Chisos Mountains (the Basin, Laguna Meadow, and Boot Canyon): Ava Nelson reported a pair at Rio Grande Village on April 18, 1979; Tommy Michael and Bob Honig saw a lone male at Cottonwood Campground on May 18, 1983; and Jerry Strickling found one at Rio Grande Village on May 12, 1962.

Palm Warbler

Dendroica palmarum

Six park records.

Joe Lunn, Martin Bovey, and I found a bird of the yellow race at Boquillas Crossing on April 1, 1970; it was collected and represents the first for the Trans-Pecos. Palm Warblers were next reported by Mrs. J. R. Barnwell, who found two at Rio Grande Village on October 14, 1972. Ben Feltner reported one for the Chisos Basin on May 5, 1980. And on May 9, 1980, Jim Shiflett and C. C. Wiedenfeld, who were leading a Chihuahuan Desert Research Institute field trip, reported finding this species at three locations: Rio Grande Village, Cottonwood Campground, and the Old Sam Nail Ranch.

Bay-breasted Warbler

Dendroica castanea

Four records for the park.

It was first reported by Albertine Bauguess and McRae Williams, who found six individuals with a wave of warblers and kinglets at Rio Grande Village on November 24, 1973. A lone female was reported there on May 10, 1978, by "D. & D. W.," a sighting considered valid at park headquarters. David Johnson next reported one at Glenn Spring on May 14, 1979, and Geth and Ed White reported a lone male at the Old Sam Nail Ranch on April 11, 1980.

Blackpoll Warbler

Dendroica striata

Four park records.

Carl Swenson first reported one along the river at Rio Grande Village on May 5, 1960;

Dave and Ginger Harwood found one flycatching over the Rio Grande Village silt pond on April 26, 1970; I observed one among the oaks at Boot Spring on May 8, 1970; and Greg and Becky Lasley and Chuck Sexton found one male at Rio Grande Village on May 15, 1979.

Black-and-white Warbler

Mniotilta varia

Uncommon migrant (March 20–May 29, August 26–October 5); rare in summer and winter.

All of the wintertime reports are from the lowlands at Rio Grande Village or near Santa Elena Canyon. It has been recorded every month but February and June.

American Redstart

Setophaga ruticilla

Fairly common migrant (March 28–June 27, August 21–September).

There is one July report: a male seen at Rio Grande Village on July 13, 1978, by Joe Buckman and Burk Gurney. There are two late fall sightings: I found a lone juvenile at Rio Grande Village on October 17, 1970, and Russ and Marian Wilson and I found one at Cottonwood Campground on October 24, 1970. There is also a single February report: David Steadman located one at Rio Grande Village on February 7 and 8, 1981.

Northbound birds reach their peak from May 1 to 23; early and late birds are either females or immature males, but most of the mid- of the spring records are from the lowlands. Fall migrants reach the Big Bend as early as August 8, and a peak is evident from September 5 to 26. Most fall birds are either females or immatures.

Prothonotary Warbler

Protonotaria citrea

Two park records.

Forrest and Aline Romero photographed one in the Basin Campground on April 27, 1971. In spite of the strange location, the photograph is that of an adult Prothonotary Warbler, perched on a Mexican piñon. It also was reported by Malcolm Otis on April 12 and 13, 1977, at Rio Grande Village.

Worm-eating Warbler

Helmitheros vermivorus

Uncommon spring migrant (April 12–May 21).

The first park record is that of a lone, singing bird taken from the oaks in upper Boot Canyon on May 4, 1967 (Wauer). The majority of the sightings are from the lowlands.

Ovenbird

Seiurus aurocapillus

Rare spring migrant (April 29–June 2).

The April 29 sighting was made at Boot Spring in 1983 by Bruce Talbot; the June 2 sighting at Boot Spring in 1976 by John Egbert. There is one earlier sighting in the Chisos Basin, on March 31, 1977, of a singing bird, by M. D. McGhee. There is also a single fall sighting of two birds on the Rio Grande Village Nature Trail on September 11, 1970 (Wauer).

Northern Waterthrush

Seiurus noveboracensis

Uncommon spring migrant (April 20–May 20); rare fall migrant (August 22–September 17).

Spring records range in location from the river floodplain to the upper Chisos canyons. This species is usually seen alone, but I found three birds at Boot Spring on May 4, 1967. It may be more common in spring than records indicate; from May 3 to 17, 1970, I captured and banded four individuals in twelve net-hours at Rio Grande Village. During the same period of days, I saw only one other Northern Waterthrush. Most fall records are from the last ten days of August. The latest record is a specimen obtained after it flew into the glass door of the Panther Junction Visitor Center on September 17, 1977 (Margaret Littlejohn).

Louisiana Waterthrush

Seiurus motacilla

Five park records (March 26–July 14).

The first park record is of a lone bird seen near Boquillas Crossing on March 27, 1970 (Wauer). John Miller next reported one at Rio Grande Village on May 6, 1976. Tyrrel Harvey, Steve Hawkins, and Richard Schaefer saw one at Boot Spring on July 12, 1980, and Eric Scholz found one at Cottonwood Campground two days later. Doug Overacker reported one at Rio Grande Village on March 26, 1981.

Kentucky Warbler

Oporornis formosus

Sporadic spring migrant (March 17–May 11).

This ground warbler has been reported for the park only since 1975. The first record is from the Chisos Basin on May 8, 1975, by Mary Davidson. There were six reports in 1976: J. Mark Rowland found one at the Old Sam Nail Ranch on March 17 and 18; R. L. Hooper reported one at Dugout Wells on March 19 that was seen there again the following day by J. Mark Rowland and Doris and Julian Darden. One was found at Rio Grande Village on March 30 by Scott Robinson, and Ed and Martha Curry reported one at Dugout Wells on May 6. The next series of sightings was in 1980: O. R. Henderson found one in the Chisos Basin on April 29; Ben Feltner found one there on May 5; Jim Shiflett observed one on the Window Trail on May 7; and Jim and Dennis Rogers reported one female at Rio Grande Village on May 11.

Mourning Warbler

Oporornis philadelphia

One park record.

On April 18, 1972, I saw this bird along the Rio Grande Village Nature Trail.

MacGillivray's Warbler

Oporornis tolmiei

Common spring migrant (April 8–May 27); rare fall migrant (August 31–September 14).

This bird may be numerous along the river floodplain from late April to mid-May. Although most sightings are from the lowlands, it has been recorded in the mountains on a number of occasions.

Common Yellowthroat

Geothlypis trichas

Fairly common summer resident at localized areas along the river; common migrant and winter resident.

Nesting birds find suitable habitats in reeds and tules along the river and adjacent ponds. A few pairs nest regularly at the silt pond and the beaver pond at Rio Grande Village; two youngsters were seen at the silt pond on July 9, 1968 (Wauer). In migration it is most numerous along the river, but it also has been reported from water areas throughout the park; for example, C. Philip Allen found one at Boot Canyon on July 31, 1963, and I observed one at Oak Spring on September 9, 1967. Wintering birds can usually be found at areas of heavy vegetation all along the floodplain.

Hooded Warbler

Wilsonia citrina

Rare spring migrant (April 30–May 18).

There is a midsummer report of a singing bird at Laguna Meadow on June 16, 1979, by Ann Ayers and Marge Eaton. All of the spring reports are from the lowlands, except for an observation in upper Pine Canyon on April 30, 1969 (Wauer). There are two additional records: I found one bird at Rio Grande Village on September 1, 1971, and Bill Bromberg and Dr. Gordon Baumgartner reported one at Boquillas on November 21, 1961.

Wilson's Warbler

Wilsonia pusilla

Abundant migrant (March 28–June 4, August 8–October 12) from the river floodplain to the top of the Chisos Mountains.

This is the park's most common migrant. A few birds reach the area by March 28, and by the second week in April it becomes abundant. A peak is reached from April 22 to 27: more than 85 individuals were counted in mesquites within one 125-square-foot area at Rio Grande Village on April 22, 1970, and more than 40 were found at Hot Springs on April 27, 1967 (Wauer). The majority of spring migrants pass through the area by May 20. The peak of the fall migration is reached from August 30 to September 19. There is a single winter sighting of one bird at Rio Grande Village on December 27, 1976, by Tris Wiedenfeld.

Canada Warbler

Wilsonia canadensis

Four park records.

David Wolf first observed a lone female feeding in low, damp brush near the corral at Boot Spring on August 23, 1966. Charles and Ella Newell next found one at Rio Grande Village on May 7, 1971. On August 28, 1977, Louis Yorke reported a male at Laguna Meadow, and on May 19, 1978, Ian McGregor found a male above the Basin Campground. Additionally, Bonnie McKinney reported one at Black Gap Wildlife Management Area, just north of the park, on October 9, 1982.

Red-faced Warbler

Cardellina rubrifrons

Sporadic summer visitor to the Chisos Mountains.

It was first reported by Bruce A. Mack at Boot Spring, on June 5, 1964, but I listed it as a hypothetical in the first edition of this book. Robert Anderson next reported one from Boot Spring on August 10, 1973. And in 1974, Glenn Britt reported one near the Basin sewage lagoons on June 5. Then, in 1978, it was reported for Boot Spring on two occasions: H. P. Langridge found one on July 9, and Wendy Watson, Gene Warren, and Garry Spence saw one on August 16. Also in 1978, Julius W. Dieckert observed and photographed one in lower Boot Canyon on August 10. And in 1983, M. Stewart found one there on August 28.

This is a bird of the Southwestern mountains, and its presence in the Chisos, several hundred miles east of its known breeding range, should be carefully monitored. Since the habitat within the Chisos Mountains seems similar to that of its known breeding habitat in southern New Mexico, these increasing records may suggest an eastern movement of the breeding population. This colorful bird would be a welcome addition to the Big Bend Country.

Painted Redstart

Myioborus pictus

Local summer resident in the higher canyons of the Chisos Mountains.

Van Tyne and Sutton (1937) reported that there appeared to be "great fluctuations in the numbers" of this bird, and that "in [June] 1901 [Vernon] Bailey, [Louis Agassiz] Fuertes, and [Harry C.] Oberholser saw no Painted Redstarts during their three weeks' exploration of these mountains [the Chisos]. In 1928, Van Tyne and [Frederick M. and Helen T.] Gaige found the species fairly numerous at Boot Spring, and yet Van Tyne, [Max M.] Peet, and [Edouard C.] Jacot spent the whole of May at the same locality four years later without getting more than an unsatisfactory glimpse of one; and the Carnegie Museum party, in 1933 and 1935, did not record the species at all. On June 24, 1936, however, Tarleton Smith saw an adult male at the head of Blue Creek Canyon." And on May 13, 1937, H. W. Brandt found a nest with three eggs at Boot Spring. That record was the first documentation of breeding for the Chisos Mountains and Texas.

There were no further reports of Painted Redstarts for the park until Harold Brodrick found several at Boot Spring on April 3, 1958. There were five records during the 1960s: Ralph Raitt found it in Pine Canyon on April 16, 1961; David and Roy Brown reported it at Boot Spring on April 28, 1966; David Simon found one there on August 27, 1966; I observed two singing birds in Oak Creek, just below the Basin Campground, on March 19, 1967; and Rena Ross, Thelma Fox, Mary Griffith, Margarite Hollar, and Peggy Accord reported one for Boot Spring on May 12, 1969. I found singing birds in Boot Canyon on April 10, 18, and 24, 1971. And then there was another period of no records.

Since 1976, Painted Redstarts have been reported for the Boot Canyon area every year but 1979. John Egbert, who spent May and June 1976 in Boot Canyon studying the Colima Warbler, reported Painted Redstarts from May 18 on, and on June 19, he found a nest with four eggs in a grass clump under a mountain sage. Park records show that 1977 was a good Painted Redstart year: Warren Pulich found a pair with two young out of the nest at Boot Spring on July 8, and David and Mimi Wolf reported two fairly young birds at Boot Spring on July 23 and 24; Chuck Hunter, Rich Pruett, and Wesley Cureton found seven birds in Boot Canyon on August 9; and Andrew Stewart and Ron and

Painted Redstart, *Myioborus pictus*

Marcia Brown reported three adults and one immature bird there on September 4. In 1978, Scott (1978) wrote that "for the third consecutive year," this bird was "common in moist canyons of the high Chisos," and "several widely singing birds were found May 20." There were several records again during 1980 and 1981, and in 1982, Greg Lasley reported that the species was "more common this year than last." Joe Kuban found six singing males in Boot Canyon on March 18, 1982; and Bruce and Chris Palmer found a nest with four eggs there on May 13, 1982. And 1983 was again a good Painted Redstart year in the Chisos.

In addition to the above records, there are two lowland sightings: Captain and Mrs. E. B. Hurlbert, Becky Wauer, and I found one at Rio

Grande Village on March 20, 1971, and Abbot and Ava Nelson reported a lone male there on March 17, 1978.

This is a common nesting bird of the forested slopes of the Maderas del Carmen Mountains of Coahuila, Mexico, fifty miles southeast of the Chisos. It apparently has become a regular breeding bird of the Chisos Mountains.

Rufous-capped Warbler

Basileuterus rufifrons

Extremely rare visitor to the park.

This little Mexican warbler has been recorded in the United States only at Big Bend National Park, in the vicinity of Falcon Dam in Texas, and in southern Arizona at Cave Creek Canyon. It was first observed in Texas by John Rowlett and Victor Emanuel on February 10, 1973, below Falcon Dam but was not seen again. On September 9, 1973, David Wolf discovered one in Campground Canyon in the Chisos Basin. It was next seen in the same location in May 1974; Byron Berger, Jerry and Nancy Strickling, Rose Ann Rowlett, and I observed it on May 24. And there were numerous records during June and July, including observations by David Easterla, Joe Taylor, Paul Sykes, William Biggs, Larry Hobkins, Dave Goodwin, and Ed Kutac. It was seen again during July and August and as late as November 23 (Ben Feltner) in 1975, in the same general area.

Then, in 1976, it was discovered along the Santa Elena Canyon Nature Trail on August 3 by Timothy Thomas and seen independently by Jack Whetstone. It was seen there again on April 15, 1977, by Burnell Hill and Laurie Schaetzel, and recorded by an additional 26 individuals during the next two weeks. It was not seen again during 1976 but was reported sporadically in 1978: Travis Beck found it on the Santa Elena Canyon Nature Trail on January 27, and Mary Shannon reported it there on December 17. In 1979, it was seen there by numerous birders between March 23 and May 5. At the end of 1984 there had been no further reports.

This is a common warbler of "open woodlands, brushy hillsides, rarely forests; foothills into mts. (to 7000 ft.)" (Peterson and Chalif, 1973) in Mexico, although I have not found it in the Maderas del Carmen Mountains, 50 miles south of the Chisos. Victor Emanuel informed me that Mike Braun found seventy Rufous-capped Warblers in the Fraile Mountains, 45 miles south of Falcon Dam, on July 4, 1974. This species is likely to occur again within the park, and the chances that it might become established as a breeding bird are good.

Yellow-breasted Chat

Icteria virens

Abundant summer resident; uncommon in migration.

This large warbler is abundant along the river floodplain and less numerous at riparian areas, such as Dugout Wells and the Old Sam Nail Ranch, up to 4,000 feet in elevation. It has been recorded from April 10 through September 24, and there is a late sighting of one bird at Boquillas Crossing on November 3, 1967 (Wauer). Early spring arrivals are quiet, but by the end of April this is the most vociferous bird of the floodplain. Displaying birds can be found every few dozen feet wherever there is a heavy growth of vegetation from Lajitas to Stillwell Crossing. By the end of July there is some dispersal of early nesters, but others are still feeding young. In mid-August a definite decrease in chats is evident, and they are almost entirely gone from their breeding territories by the end of the month. Most September sightings are of late nesters and migrants. There apparently is

Yellow-breasted Chat, *Icteria virens*

some movement through the mountains; Walter Boles, Jim Shields, and John St. Julien found a lone bird at Boot Spring on August 10, 1970. There are no other records above 4,000 feet.

Olive Warbler

Peucedramus taeniatus

Four park records.

Charles Bender and Bill Mealy found one first near the South Rim on August 19, 1966. I found a lone bird in Boot Canyon on September 19, 1970; Thelma Dalmas reported one at Laguna Meadow on July 4, 1975; and Robert Harms reported one on the Window Trail January 4, 1979. This species is a fairly common breeding bird in the forested highlands of the Maderas del Carmen Mountains, fifty miles southeast of the park, and postnesting birds should be expected.

Tanagers: *Family Emberizidae, Subfamily Thraupinae*

Hepatic Tanager

Piranga flava

Uncommon summer resident (April 19–September 25) above 5,000 feet in the Chisos Mountains.

There is one late record at Boot Spring by Gene Blacklock and Bruce Fall on October 19, 1974. Although this species is never numerous, it occurs regularly at a few localities. Pairs can usually be found just above the Basin cottages and along the start of the South Rim Trail, in the vicinity of Juniper Flat and the water storage tank, along the second mile of the South Rim Trail, along the Colima Trail just above Laguna Meadow, and near the upper water barrel in Green Gulch. Singing birds can be heard from the Basin cottages almost any morning in May. I found a nest on a piñon pine near the Chisos Mountains Lodge on May 12, 1968, and saw an adult male carrying food near there on June 10, 1967. Lowland records are questionable; I have never found this tanager below the Chisos woodlands. Fall birds can be very confusing because the bill color of the Summer Tanager is sometimes very dark in fall; the liver-red color of the Hepatic Tanager male is the only positive field characteristic at that time.

Summer Tanager

Piranga rubra

Abundant summer resident at Rio Grande Village and Cottonwood Campground and less numerous elsewhere on the floodplain and at riparian areas up to 5,000 feet.

Males arrive as early as April 1, and females and subadults follow within a week or two. By the last week of April this species is abundant at Rio Grande Village; I counted forty there on April 23, 1967. It does not reach its breeding territories in the mountain canyons until late April. It nests along the river and at such places as Dugout Wells, the Old Sam Nail Ranch, and within the deciduous vegetation along the lower canyons—for example, at Cattail Falls, in Oak Creek Canyon, and in Green Gulch. During the summers of 1968 and 1969 the feeding territories of this species and the Hepatic Tanager overlapped along the drainage of Oak Creek just below the Basin Campground.

Summer Tanagers are very gregarious and, like the Orchard and Hooded Orioles that use the same cottonwood groves at Rio Grande Village, spend a great deal of time chasing each other around the grove when they first arrive. Nesting gets under way by early May, and young are out of the nest in June, although there is some late nesting as well; nest-building was found at Rio Grande Village on June 20, 1967, and adults were seen feeding young in the nest at Boquillas Crossing on August 20, 1970 (Wauer). I have detected only minor postnesting wandering; for the most part, this species seems to remain on the breeding grounds throughout August and most of September. There is a noticeable decrease in birds by the last of September, and I could find only two individuals at Rio Grande Village on October 5, 1969. The latest sighting is of a lone bird along Oak Creek on October 10, 1967 (Wauer).

Scarlet Tanager

Piranga olivacea

Rare spring and summer vagrant (April 26–July 17).

Records range from the Rio Grande floodplain to Dugout Wells and the Old Sam Nail Ranch, and there is one sighting at the Basin on July 14, 1975, by Richard Palmer.

Western Tanager

Piranga ludoviciana

Rare in summer; fairly common migrant.

Smith (1936) reported seeing "young birds able to fly" in Pine Canyon on July 24, 1936. There is no recent evidence that this is a breeding bird of the Chisos Mountains, in spite of a vigorously singing adult male seen at Juniper Flat on June 7, 1970 (Wauer). Northbound birds may reach the Big Bend area as early as late February; Anne LeSassier and C. Philip Allen found two males on the Window Trail on February 27, 1963. There are no March records, but this bird becomes regular after April 18. Spring migrants reach a peak from May 6 to 15, and stragglers have been recorded as late as May 26. Except for the one June sighting mentioned above, there are no other park records until July 4, when postnesting or nonbreeding birds become regular in occurrence. I found adult males at Rio Grande Village on July 4, 1969, and July 12, 1970. It is more common within the mountains, where birds can be found throughout the rest of the summer. Southbound birds have been

Western Tanager, *Piranga ludoviciana*

recorded regularly during September and decrease in early October; stragglers have been recorded until October 25. There is a solitary wintertime record for Rio Grande Village on February 10, 1979 (Keith and Jan Wiggers).

Cardinals, Grosbeaks, Buntings: *Family Emberizidae, Subfamily Cardinalinae*

Northern Cardinal

Cardinalis cardinalis

Common resident in summer and winter at localized areas along the floodplain (such as the Rio Grande Village Nature Trail), and less numerous elsewhere along the river and at adjacent riparian areas up to 3,500 feet; uncommon migrant.

Breeding birds can also be found some summers at Dugout Wells, Government Spring, and the Old Sam Nail Ranch. Most sightings away from the river and other water areas are probably migrants. Small flocks of ten to fifteen birds were seen moving north near Rio Grande Village on March 21, 1969; a lone male was found at Panther Junction on March 19, 1967; and two females were seen at Government Spring on March 20, 1971 (Wauer). Hank Schmidt saw a Northern Cardinal at Panther Junction on September 16, 1960; one stayed there from November 29, 1967, to December 13, 1968, and was banded on December 9 (Wauer).

Pyrrhuloxia

Cardinalis sinuatus

Common summer and winter resident; uncommon migrant.

This is a bird of the desert washes; the look-alike Northern Cardinal prefers riparian areas. Pyrrhuloxias can usually be found at mesquite-acacia thickets along the drier parts of the floodplain and in arroyos and canyons up to 4,500 feet. Lowland birds are mostly permanent residents. Nesting occurs in April, May, and June; I found adults feeding young at Rio Grande Village on May 21, 1968, and a nest seven feet up in a mesquite there on June 14, 1968. Pyrrhuloxias are fairly shy while nesting but become easy to find again right afterward. Except among the resident birds of the floodplain, there appears to be considerable wandering after nesting. These birds become quite numerous at Panther Junction and in the Chisos Basin during late July and August. By October, birds may be found in the higher parts of the mountains as well; I saw two in upper Boot Canyon on October 22, 1967, and one near the South Rim on November 4, 1967. Wintering records are all below 5,000 feet. Most resident birds congregate in flocks of ten to thirty birds from late September through the first of March. Those in the lower mountain canyons seldom flock, but are usually found in groups of three or four.

Pyrrhuloxia, *Cardinalis sinuatus*

Rose-breasted Grosbeak

Pheucticus ludovicianus

Rare spring migrant (March 23–June 11).

It is most common May 6 to 20. The majority of the records are from the mountains, at Boot Canyon, Laguna Meadow, and Oak Creek, but there also are a number of lowland sightings.

Black-headed Grosbeak

Pheucticus melanocephalus

Common summer resident in the mountains; uncommon migrant.

This is a bird of the deciduous woodlands above 4,500 feet. It reaches the Big Bend the last week of April and begins to nest almost immediately; I found it nest-building in the Chisos Basin on May 2, 1967, and Smith (1936) reported a nest with two well-feathered young in the Basin on July 11, 1936. Breeding birds begin to move out of the area by early September, and by the middle of the month only migrants can be found. I found a late southbound bird along the Window Trail on October 4, 1968, and an immature bird visited my feeder at Panther Junction on November 4 and 5, 1969. One seen by Theodore M. Sperry and Gladys C. Galliger in the Basin on December 21, 1960, was a very late vagrant. Most of the park's Black-headed Grosbeak records are from the mountains, but there are a handful of sightings from the lowlands; I found lone males at Rio Grande Village on May 8, 1968, May 6, 1970, September 14, 1969, September 19, 1968, and September 26, 1969.

Black-headed Grosbeak, *Pheucticus melanocephalus*

Blue Grosbeak

Guiraca caerulea

Fairly common summer resident; uncommon migrant.

Like the Black-headed Grosbeak of the

mountains, this species is one of the late spring arrivals. Migrants begin to move along the Rio Grande by mid-April (the earliest record is April 16), but they do not become regular until the first of May. The Blue Grosbeak nests in riparian thickets along the river, at a few of the dense mesquite bosques in desert arroyos, and along mountain drainages to 5,000 feet. It can almost always be found in summer along the Rio Grande Village Nature Trail, at the Old Sam Nail Ranch, and along Oak Creek below the Basin Campground. Nest-building was recorded at Rio Grande Village on June 10, 1970 (David Easterla). By early August, many of the brightly colored males are in molt. This, combined with the worn plumage, makes for very mottled birds looking very much like the juveniles that trail after the adults as they feed in weedy patches adjacent to the thickets. The breeding grounds may appear practically deserted because of the birds' habit of feeding elsewhere. Fall migrants begin to replace resident birds during the last week of August and reach a peak the first few days of September. Stragglers continue to pass through the area until October 1.

Lazuli Bunting

Passerina amoena

Rare migrant (May 1–12 and accidental afterward through June 9).

The majority of the sightings are from the lowlands, but it has also been recorded in the Chisos Basin along the Window Trail, often in the company of Indigo Buntings. There are two fall records: I found three males near Santa Elena Canyon on September 2, 1968, and one was reported from Pine Canyon on September 29, 1956.

Indigo Bunting

Passerina cyanea

Uncommon spring migrant.

The earliest sighting is from Rio Grande Village on March 10, 1978, by A. Brander and H. Schultz, but most sightings are made from April 14 through May. It is rare during June, and there are a number of sightings throughout July. There appear to be two separate spring movements through the Big Bend. The first series of records range from mid-April to about May 13; there are no sightings from May 14 to 17; and another movement is evident from May 18 to 26. There are only a few records during the last few days of May and the first half of June, then there is a ten-day period when it is more numerous again.

Many of the late June sightings are of singing birds. Those found along the Window Trail appear to be competing for territories with Varied Buntings, which are very vocal in the area during this period; maybe the presence of singing Varied Buntings holds the Indigo Buntings longer. In 1970, singing male Indigos were found at Rio Grande Village from May 22 to June 10, in the same area as singing Painted Buntings. Indigos apparently vacate both areas during July. There are two later sightings: Stanley Auker reported a male at the Basin Campground on August 18, 1981, and I found an immature male at Rio Grande Village on September 18, 1970.

Varied Bunting

Passerina versicolor

Fairly common summer resident and spring migrant; four winter records.

The earliest spring records include an adult male seen at Rio Grande Village on April 4, 1972 (Wauer and Russ and Marian Wilson), and one caught in a mist net at Panther Junction on April 18, 1969; it was banded and released. During the first two weeks of May, Varied Buntings become fairly common over the desert, particularly along washes and at weedy places along the roads. Males apparently arrive on their breeding grounds first and are later followed by the females; on April 29, 1970, I found four singing males along the Window Trail, but no females. A male was actively defending a territory in this same area on May 24, 1968, and a male was seen feeding two youngsters there on July 19, 1969. I found a nest with three young in Blue Creek Canyon on June 4, 1968, and seven singing males within one mile of Cottonwood Wash, just behind the Old Sam Nail Ranch, on July 13, 1968. Four singing males and one nest on a squaw-bush were found along one mile of Blue Creek Canyon, just above the Wilson Ranch house, on June 4, 1968. It also can be found in summer in the little wash just below Government Spring, and on June 5, 1970, I found four singing birds among the rather open mesquite thickets north of the roadway northeast of Todd Hill.

There seems to be double-brooding or late nesting as well. I found an adult male feeding two fledged young along the Window Trail on August 28, 1966; and on August 23, 1970, I found nine singing males and several females and immature birds along a two-mile stretch of lower Panther Canyon. A visit there on September 13 turned up only two adult males, but one was feeding three very recently fledged youngsters.

The Varied Bunting seems to be quite numerous during wet years but less common during years of little precipitation. During the wet summer of 1968, I found a singing male within a thicket of mesquite and reeds along the river, just two miles below Santa Elena Canyon. And on August 11, 1971, Red and Marjorie Adams and Roseann Rose found an adult male feeding young below the Santa Elena Canyon Overlook There appears to be some postnesting wandering along the washes, but the bird can usually be found with some searching in the proper habitat until mid-September. In winter, Rick LoBello found with some searching in the proper habitat until mid-September.

In winter, Rick LoBello found one at the Old Sam Nail Ranch on December 3, 1976; I found a lone adult male just below the Basin Campground on December 28, 1968; Glenn Cureton reported a male behind the stables in the Basin on December 30, 1976; and Jesse Boyce and Cathy Moitoret reported one at Santa Elena on February 22, 1976.

Painted Bunting

Passerina ciris

Abundant summer resident at Rio Grande Village, common elsewhere along the floodplain and less numerous at springs and water areas up to 3,500 feet; rare spring migrant.

This is another rather late spring arrival; the earliest sighting is April 4 (David Easterla), but it is not until April 24 that it becomes suddenly common along the floodplain. Nesting occurs during June, July, and August, but males move away from their breeding territories during the first two weeks of August. Only female and immature birds are usually seen afterward. By early September, females and young are also often hard to find, but a search through weed patches at Rio Grande Village will usually turn up a few. Immature birds can usually be found at such places until October 5.

Fall migrants are rare; an adult male found on the Rio Grande Village Nature Trail on September 21, 1970, was assumed to be a migrant because it was the first adult male seen there since August 22. There is also an extremely late sighting of a lone female at Rio Grande Village on November 19, 1970 (Wauer). Spring migrants are somewhat more numerous; I found lone birds at the Old Sam Nail Ranch on May 4 and 23, 1968, and banded an adult female at Panther Junction on May 21, 1970.

Dickcissel

Spiza americana

Uncommon migrant (April 26–May 27, August 17–October 15).

There were no records of this bird prior to 1967, when one appeared at my feeder at Panther Junction on May 14. Since then I have found it regularly. Three were banded at Panther Junction in 1967, on September 7, 8, and 10; none in 1968; two in 1969, on August 29 and September 1; five at Rio Grande Village on September 20, 1969; and none in 1970. Most records are of small flocks of two to five birds. I cannot help wondering whether this species did not move through the Big Bend previously or was just missed in earlier years.

Towhees, Sparrows, Longspurs: *Family Emberizidae, Subfamily Emberizinae*

Green-tailed Towhee

Pipilo chlorurus

Fairly common migrant and winter resident.

Smith (1936) reported a nest containing eggs from 4,500 feet in the Chisos Basin on July 10, 1936. The only other evidence of nesting is an apparently territorial bird seen above Laguna Meadow, May 28, 1971, by Ted Parker and Harold Morrin. The bird reaches the Big Bend area as early as September 19 in fall but does not become common until mid-October, when it may be numerous along the arroyos below 5,000 feet. Fall migration subsides by early November, but stragglers and winter residents can usually be found at thickets almost everywhere below the piñon-juniper-oak woodlands.

The Green-tailed Towhee can most easily be found at the Old Sam Nail Ranch and Dugout Wells, although it is also present throughout winter and spring along the floodplain and at washes near Panther Junction. The population begins to increase about mid-March as northbound birds enter the area. The spring migration, usually greater than the fall movement, reaches a peak during the second week of April. There is a slight lapse in sightings during mid-April, followed by another increase from April 24 to May 6, and stragglers continue to pass through the area until May 17.

Rufous-sided Towhee

Pipilo erythrophthalmus

Fairly common permanent resident in the mountains; uncommon migrant and winter resident elsewhere.

Nesting birds are confined to the wooded canyons of the Chisos Mountains and nest during May, June, July, and August. The majority seem to remain in their breeding territories throughout the year; one banded at Boot Spring on January 26 was recaptured there again on May 7. Some fall dispersal is evident in September, when high-country birds apparently move into the lower canyons. Fall migrants have not been recorded until the middle of October; the earliest sighting along the river is one at Rio Grande Village on October 18. This bird then becomes regular at localized places throughout the winter. Spring migrants come to the Big Bend area by mid-March, reach a peak during the second week of April, and have been recorded only once after April 21: one at Rio Grande Village on May 15, 1968 (Wauer).

Brown Towhee

Pipilo fuscus

Abundant resident of the sotol grasslands and less numerous in the higher mountains and within the lower arroyos.

Rufous-sided Towhee, *Pipilo erythrophthalmus*

This is the plain brown bird that is numerous in the Basin Campground and around the cottages. Nesting occurs from April throughout the summer and fall during wet years; in 1966, I found an adult bird feeding a spotted youngster on the Lost Mine Trail on November 6. There seems to be some altitudinal movement during some winters; it was recorded at Rio Grande Village from September 21 through April in 1969–70, but I have not found it there during other winters.

Brown Towhee, *Pipilo fuscus*

Cassin's Sparrow

Aimophila cassinii

Common summer resident in wet years (may be completely absent in dry years); fairly common migrant; uncommon winter resident.

This is one of Big Bend's most fascinating sparrows because of its almost complete dependence upon the spring and summer rainy season for nesting. It is a regular nesting sparrow of the grasslands in northern Brewster County and north to Fort Stockton and Fort Davis; I have found singing birds along the highways every May, June, and July, and in wet years during August and September.

It is a very sporadic nesting bird within the park, however. In 1967, 3 skylarking males were observed in lower Green Gulch on June 3, and 15 singing birds were counted there on July 30, several days after heavy showers. In 1968, cool and moist weather prevailed from April through September. A few singing birds were heard in Green Gulch as early as June 27, and an estimated 35 skylarking birds were counted there on July 4. The summer of 1969 was exceptionally dry. Cassin's Sparrows were found singing at a few places in spring, but searches for nesting birds in Green Gulch in June, July, and August proved fruitless, although 5 to 7 individuals were found singing on Dog Canyon Flat on June 6. In 1970, I did not find any singing birds during the relatively dry spring and early summer, but after some rainy periods in July and August, the Cassin's Sparrow became the most numerous singing bird of the grassy areas of the park below 4,000 feet. In fact, skylarking birds were seen in numbers at Rio Grande Village and along the River Road all during August; I found an estimated 30 singing birds along the River Road on August 21. Most of these birds had left the area by mid-September, but many remained at grassy places throughout the fall and winter.

Peter Scott reported that 1979, from March to early June, was a good year for Cassin's Sparrows.

In drier years, when nesting birds are not already numerous in August and September, there is a distinct movement of migrants into the park during the first week of September. This burst of migrants is over by September 20. Wintering birds can usually be found at choice weedy places along the river, such as old fields at Castolon and Rio Grande Village. A high count of 58 birds was recorded on the Chisos Mountains Christmas Count of December 28, 1968. Singing begins during the second week of March at the wintering areas, but these birds are soon replaced with spring migrants. There are only a few sightings from mid-April to June 25, but this lapse apparently depends solely upon the precipitation, because as soon as the rains begin it is only a few days before singing birds can be found.

Rufous-crowned Sparrow

Aimophila ruficeps

Common permanent resident of the sotol grasslands and less numerous within the piñon-juniper-oak woodlands and the upper desert arroyos.

This species is static in its occurrence; a bird banded at Boot Spring on January 26, 1968, was seen there on February 23 and May 8, 1968, and on June 7, 1970 (Wauer). Nesting occurs during April and May and again during the summer rainy period in July, August, and September. In fact, in the lower part of the bird's range, nesters are much more active during wet summers than in spring. The Chisos Mountains Christmas Counts tallied 47 individuals in 1966, 129 in 1967, 110 in 1968, 16 in 1969, and 83 in 1970.

Chipping Sparrow

Spizella passerina

Common migrant and fairly common winter visitor.

Pansy Espy reports that it nests in the Davis Mountains. This is probably the park's most numerous sparrow from October to mid-May. It has been recorded every month but June. There is a lapse of sightings from May 26 to July 19, on which date in 1970 a postnesting bird was caught, banded, and released at Panther Junction. This sparrow does not become regular in occurrence until late September. The fall movement continues through October and reaches a peak in early October, when mixed flocks of Chippers and Clay-colored Sparrows and a few Brewer's Sparrows are common along the desert roadways and floodplain. Most flocks of *Spizella* seen in the mountains are almost all Chippers.

Wintering birds are most numerous below 5,500 feet, but they can usually be found among the piñon-juniper woodlands on the South and East rims during warmer winter days. Chippers can always be found in winter near the sewage lagoons in the Basin, and small flocks are fairly common on the floodplain.

Spring migration is well under way by the third week of March. Flocks of thirty to fifty birds can often be found feeding under the cottonwoods at Rio Grande Village and Cottonwood Campground on open ground in the Chisos Basin. The northbound movement does not begin to subside until the middle of May, and stragglers have been recorded through May 25.

Clay-colored Sparrow

Spizella pallida

Sporadic migrant and winter resident (September 3–May 31).

Some years this bird is almost as numerous as the Chipping Sparrow; other years it is rare. Records are almost totally confined to the open desert and arroyos below 4,000 feet; I have found it in the mountain woodlands only a few times. In September 1968 it was abundant; only one was seen at Dugout Wells on September 10, but on the morning on September 17, thousands were found over the desert. These birds were in the company of Lark Buntings and an occasional Field or Lincoln's Sparrow. This wave of sparrows subsided by late afternoon, and I found only a few individuals in the same area on September 19. The winters of 1968–69 and 1970–71 were good "sparrow winters," and Clay-coloreds could be found at weedy fields along the river all winter.

Northbound migrants begin to move into the area by mid-March, and a peak is reached during the first week of April. Stragglers continue to pass through the park until May 4. During the 1969–70 fall, winter, and spring, the bird was recorded from September 19 through October 26; none were seen during November, December, January, and February; and only a few migrants were recorded from March 18 to May 6.

Brewer's Sparrow

Spizella breweri

Uncommon migrant and sporadic winter visitor.

Records range from October 20 through May 6. Like the Clay-colored Sparrow, the

Brewer's is rarely seen above 4,500 feet. Fall migrants are somewhat sporadic and are almost always in association with Chipping or Clay-colored Sparrows. Wintering birds can be found at weedy fields along the river during "sparrow years"; I found it during the winters of 1966–67, 1968–69, and 1970–71 at Rio Grande Village and Castolon. It was present within the sotol grasslands all of winter 1970–71 as well. During the spring migration it can be found with certainty only from mid-March through mid-April. A peak is reached from March 15 to 27, and flocks of ten to fifty birds can often be detected by their chorus of musical trills. Stragglers may be found in the park until May 6.

Field Sparrow

Spizella pusilla

Sporadic migrant and winter visitor.

Like the rest of the *Spizella,* this little sparrow may be fairly common during some winters and hard to find others. During 1967–68 it was found in numbers throughout the grassy slopes of the Chisos below 5,000 feet. A specimen was taken at Rio Grande Village on November 19, and nine individuals were banded at Panther Junction on the following dates: December 31, January 10 (two) and 15, February 3, 6, and 27, and March 15 and 17. In 1968–69, several were found along the river and in the grasslands from September 15 to March 15. But I found only one during the entire fall, winter, and spring of 1969–70, at Castolon on December 21. Field Sparrows were present in small numbers up to 4,000 feet throughout the 1970–71 winter.

Black-chinned Sparrow

Spizella atrogularis

Fairly common summer resident at chaparral areas above 5,200 feet; sporadic winter resident.

Singing birds have been recorded as early as March 17 in the Basin, where the Black-chinned can often be found along the upper part of the Window Trail and adjacent to the campground. It nests there, along the north and west slopes below Casa Grande, and on the northern slope below Laguna Meadow adjacent to the South Rim Trail. Some years it is abundant at Laguna Meadow; twelve singing birds were counted on the chaparral flat there on May 7, 1970. During dry years it apparently waits until the summer rainy season before nesting.

Wintering Black-chins may be fairly common at weedy patches in the canyons between 4,400 feet and 5,400 feet, but some winters they are difficult or impossible to find. In 1967, fifteen were found in Maple Canyon on January 20, and twelve along the Window Trail on January 21. There is a defined downward movement in winter; none have been recorded above 5,400 feet from November 6 through mid-April. If enough rain falls in the summer to produce a good grass crop, the Black-chinned can usually be found wintering along the Window Trail (just below the sewage lagoons is a good place), along the edge of the upper Basin (near the Chisos Trailhead), and at weedy patches in middle Green Gulch.

Vesper Sparrow

Pooecetes gramineus

Common migrant and fairly common winter resident.

Black-chinned Sparrow, *Spizella atrogularis*

Fall migrants reach the area as early as August 27 and become common from mid-September through October. Migrants can usually be found along the roadways and at weedy places almost everywhere below 5,400 feet, although this sparrow may be expected in the highlands as well; I found several near the East Rim on September 25, 1967. Wintering birds are generally restricted to the lower, weedy flats and seem to be somewhat sporadic in occurrence. I have found Vespers most numerous during certain "sparrow winters," such as 1967–68, when 24 individuals were banded at Panther Junction between January 13 and April 18. During that period it was, except for Chippers, the most numerous sparrow banded.

Spring migrants reach the park by mid-March; there is a peak in sightings during the first two weeks of April, and then they gradually decline until May 17.

Lark Sparrow

Chondestes grammacus

Fairly common migrant and uncommon post-nesting visitor.

This is a common nesting bird at weedy thickets along roadsides and washes of northern Brewster County. It may nest in similar places within the park; I found a lone bird at Panther Junction on June 6, 1967, and David Easterla saw one at Ernst Tinaja on June 29, 1968. Small flocks of three to ten birds begin to move into the area during the last week of July and become regular at old fields and weedy areas from mid-August until October 24; there is a peak in the fall migration from August 19 to mid-September. There are solitary November and December sightings: I found lone birds near Solis on November 11, 1967, and at Gano Spring on December 29, 1970. There are no records for January and February, but northbound migrants arrive as early as March 19. Spring migrants are most common from mid-April through May 8, and less numerous thereafter until May 18. There are a few records for the Chisos Basin, but for the most part, this species is pretty well confined to the desert and arroyos below 4,000 feet.

Black-throated Sparrow, *Amphispiza bilineata*

Black-throated Sparrow

Amphispiza bilineata

Common permanent resident of the shrub desert and less numerous along the floodplain and up to 4,200 feet in the sotol grasslands.

Nesting takes place from April to June and again in July, August, and September if the rains produce suitable seed plants. This little sparrow can be found in flocks of five to thirty birds during much of the year and can easily be detected by its tinkling calls. It is somewhat shy during nesting. Youngsters lack the typical black throats of adults. This difference may be confusing, but they are almost always accompanied by adults. Black-throats are the park's most commonly seen desert sparrow.

Sage Sparrow

Amphispiza belli

Sporadic winter visitor only.

This western species may be more common within the Big Bend than records indicate. I found a small flock in a grassy area near the upper Tornillo Creek bridge on January 5, 1969; thirteen were counted there on January 18, and one of ten seen was collected on February 11. There is one more sighting in 1969: Robert Rothstein found "a few" birds just east of Castolon on March 19. On October 24, 1970, Russ and Marian Wilson and I found a lone bird at Rio Grande Village, and Jim Tucker and Jon Barlow found three near the Nine Point Draw bridge on December 31, 1970.

Lark Bunting

Calamospiza melanocorys

Fairly common migrant (March 6–May 28, August 4–October 18); sporadic winter visitor.

There is a lapse of records only from May 29 to August 3. Fall migrants do not become regular until early September, and a peak is reached during the middle of the month. With some searching, wintering birds can usually be found around Panther Junction, Rio Grande Village, and the Castolon area. Some winters this species may be abundant, and flocks of 100 or more birds are not uncommon; 252 were banded at Panther Junction during the 1967–68 winter, none in 1968–69, 23 in 1969–70, and 52 in 1970–71. Wintering birds, as well as migrants, remain below 4,500 feet; there are no records for the Basin. Spring migrants may be numerous along the river and in desert washes from March 17 to May 7. On March 22 and 23, 1969, I saw thousands of Lark Buntings moving along the river between Boquillas and Stillwell Crossing.

Savannah Sparrow

Passerculus sandwichensis

Uncommon migrant and winter visitor.

Early fall migrants may reach the park by September 14, but this bird is most numerous during the latter part of October. Wintering birds can usually be found at weedy patches and grassy flats along the river and in the lower washes up to 4,500 feet. Spring migrants begin to move through the area by mid-March and may be quite numerous along the river. The latest sighting is at Rio Grande Village on May 24, 1967. At least two different races of Savannah Sparrows visit the park. They look considerably different, and this variation can lead to confusion; the wintering resident and early spring migrant is smaller and lighter than the large, dark form, which is a migrant only.

Baird's Sparrow

Ammodramus bairdii

Rare migrant (April 2–May 21, September 6–January 25); sporadic winter visitor.

All sightings are from weedy areas below 4,000 feet. I have found it regularly only from mid-October to late December at old fields near Castolon and at Rio Grande Village. The most productive places have been along the Santa Elena Crossing roadway and adjacent to Alamo Creek near the paved Santa Elena Canyon road.

Grasshopper Sparrow

Ammodramus savannarum

Uncommon migrant in spring and rare in fall; sporadic winter resident at grassy areas from the floodplain to the lower mountain canyons.

It has been recorded as early as September 26, but southbound birds cannot be expected with regularity. During the winter of 1967–68 this bird was present at weedy places in Green Gulch and in Panther Canyon, as well as in old fields at Castolon, from December 5 through March 19, but I could not find it at these localities the next two winters. Spring migrants pass through the park area from March 8 to April 4, and except for a lone bird in the Basin on May 18, 1967 (Wauer), sightings are all below 5,000 feet.

Le Conte's Sparrow

Ammodramus leconteii

Rare migrant and winter visitor.

There is a scattering of records from late August through the winter until early March, all from the Rio Grande floodplain. It was first found at Rio Grande Village, on March 10, 1963, by Mr. and Mrs. C. Edgar Bedell. I found one there on August 29 and two on October 24, 1966. Ben Feltner next reported one in the open fields at Castolon on January 3, 1972. David Wiedenfeld found six at San Vicente on December 27, 1976. Eric and Mildred Hartman and Carroll and Lucy McEathron reported finding fourteen individuals along the River Road on February 16, 1977. Peter Scott stated that he observed the species throughout the 1976–77 winter in the fields at San Vicente, and that the birds left the area by mid-March. There have been no recent reports.

Fox Sparrow

Passerella iliaca

Sporadic winter resident (November 1–March 15) on the Rio Grande floodplain.

John Galley first reported this bird for the park when he found a lone individual at the Santa Elena Canyon picnic area on February 1, 1967. A specimen, apparently the same individual, was taken at this locality on February 12, 1967, and proved to be the eastern race *zaboria* (Wauer, 1969*b*). I also found it on November 1 and December 17, 1967, and December 23, 1970, in similar habitats near Rio Grande Village, where it was also seen on March 15, 1974, by Glenn and Maryjane Crane and on December 27, 1976, by Wesley Cureton. Four individuals were seen there by Eric and Mildred Hartman and Lucy and Carroll McEathron on February 16, 1977; Alan Wormington and B. Wylie reported seven there on February 9; and Barbara Nielsen found it there on March 9. A. Brander and H. Schultz reported it for Rio Grande Village on March 8 and 9, 1978. Bryan Bland found another there on March 12, 1981. And on January 31, 1982, Barbara and Daniel McKnight observed one there of the eastern race.

Song Sparrow

Melospiza melodia

Uncommon migrant and rare winter visitor.

Fall birds reach the area as early as October 12, a peak is reached from October 24 to 28, and late migrants can usually be found throughout December. This species is rarely seen in January and February, but it can be found with considerable searching at swampy or weedy places along the river. Northbound birds begin to move along the river by the second week of March and become most numerous from April 1 to 11; a high of five birds was seen at Rio Grande Village on April 8, 1970 (Wauer). Stragglers have been recorded within the park until May 10.

Lincoln's Sparrow

Melospiza lincolnii

Common migrant in spring, and fairly common in fall and winter.

This perky little sparrow has been recorded within the park as early as September 15 and as late as June 1. Fall migrants reach a peak from October 19 to 26, but they can be found at weedy patches along the river and in canyons to 5,300 feet almost anytime during migration and in winter. Spring migrants become numerous from March 15 to April 11, and stragglers continue to pass through the area until late May.

Swamp Sparrow

Melospiza georgiana

Uncommon migrant and fairly common winter resident at a few localized water areas along the river.

Fall migrants do not reach the Big Bend area until October 5 and have been recorded as late as May 20. This bird is usually more common than the related Song Sparrow, which utilizes the same habitat, and can best be found at the beaver dam area and the silt pond at Rio Grande Village. Swamp Sparrows and Yellowthroats can usually be squeaked out of hiding at these places throughout the winter and spring.

The Swamp Sparrow can also be found at weedy fields below 4,500 feet during winters following wet summers.

White-throated Sparrow

Zonotrichia albicollis

Uncommon winter visitor and migrant.

Records range from November 2 to May 10. Although this species is never numerous, it occurs regularly at lowland, brushy areas during winter. I have found it most often near riparian habitats along the river, less often at higher elevations, such as Dugout Wells, Grapevine Spring, and the Old Sam Nail Ranch. It also occurs irregularly in the lower mountain canyons, such as lower Green Gulch, and along the Window Trail. In migration it can be expected anywhere below 5,000 feet.

Golden-crowned Sparrow

Zonotrichia atricapilla

Five park records.

On December 9, 1971, I captured (and banded) an immature bird found with a flock of several hundred White-crowns in the Alamo Creek drainage near Castolon. I saw it there again on December 28, and Ben Feltner observed an unbanded juvenile there on January 3, 1972. Larry May and I observed one at the Boquillas Canyon parking area on January 15, 1974; Larry obtained several slides. And Tex Sordahl reported one for the Rio Grande Village Campground on January 12, 1982.

White-crowned Sparrow

Zonotrichia leucophrys

Common migrant and winter resident below 5,000 feet.

It has been recorded from September 15 through June 4. Early fall migrants are restricted to the Rio Grande lowlands and do not appear in the higher elevations until mid-October, when the species may be common along the river, uncommon in the grasslands, and rare in the lower woodlands. Wintering birds are common all along the river but sporadic at higher elevations. During the 1966–67 winter, I banded 472 White-crowns at Panther Junction, but only 112 in 1967–68, 105 in 1968–69, none in 1969–70, and 22 in 1970–71. This species is most numerous at Rio Grande Village and Cottonwood Campground, where wintering birds may remain until late May. Spring migrants begin to move through the park area by mid-March and may be numerous along the floodplain and at adjacent mesquite bosques until mid-May. Stragglers may pass through the lowlands until June.

Harris' Sparrow

Zonotrichia querula

Three records for the park.

Captain and Mrs. E. B. Hurlbert saw one at the Santa Elena Canyon picnic area on February 25, 1965; Mr. and Mrs. C. Edgar Bedell recorded one at Rio Grande Village from February 15 to 22, 1966; and a lone adult visited my feeder at Panther Junction from November 30 to December 6, 1968. It was captured, photographed, banded, and released.

Dark-eyed Junco

Junco hyemalis

Three easily recognized forms—known as the Slate-colored, Oregon, and Gray-headed Juncos before they were lumped together by the revised AOU *Check-list* (1983)—occur in the park. Although the species as a whole may be considered a fairly common migrant and winter resident, particularly in the middle elevations of the park, I will discuss them separately here.

Slate-Colored Junco

Uncommon migrant and winter resident.

Records range from October 20 to March 25. It has been recorded from the river floodplain up to Boot Canyon, but the only place I have found it consistently is along the Window Trail between December 1 and March 25. It is almost always seen either alone or with a small flock of Oregons or Gray-heads; two or three Slate-colored Juncos are only rarely found together.

Oregon Junco

Fairly common migrant and winter resident in the mountains and less numerous elsewhere.

It arrives as early as October 20 and has not been reported after April 6. Most sightings are of one to eight birds along the Window Trail or at Boot Spring, and migrants are often in association with Slate-colored and Gray-headed Juncos.

Gray-headed Junco

Uncommon migrant and fairly common winter resident.

Fall birds arrive as early as mid-October, and the latest spring record is John Egbert's sighting of one at Boot Spring on June 11, 1976. On May 27, 1968, I banded 5 birds from a flock of about 25 at Boot Spring, where I had previously recorded the same flock on October 22,

1967, February 13 and 23, 1968, and March 31, 1968. Three birds of this same flock were recaptured at Boot Spring on October 20, 1968. The flock remained until at least May 9. This is the most numerous wintering junco in the mountains.

Chestnut-collared Longspur

Calcarius ornatus

Rare spring migrant.

It was first reported by Thompson G. March, who found a lone bird atop the South Rim, walking along the trail in front of him, on March 25, 1960. Captain E. B. Hurlbert observed one on Tornillo Flat on April 5, 1961. There were no other park records until 1970, when an immature male was taken at my feeder at Panther Junction on March 13, and a group of four was seen there on March 12, 20, 23, and 24. It was next reported on February 15, 1976, a few miles north of Panther Junction (park records). There are several 1983 records: Bonnie McKinney banded one male at Black Gap Wildlife Management Area headquarters on February 10; she observed one female and one immature bird there on February 25; and she banded and photographed another male that was taken from a mist net (where it was singing) at the same locality on May 27, 1983. And Bruce Talbot reported thirty birds (three of which were males) along the River Road near La Clocha on March 17, 1983.

Blackbirds, Orioles: *Family Emberizidae, Subfamily Icterinae*

Red-winged Blackbird

Agelaius phoeniceus

Uncommon migrant and possibly a breeding bird at suitable localities along the Rio Grande.

It is most numerous in migration from mid-April through mid-May in spring, and from late August through mid-September in fall; it has been recorded in every month but December and January. There is one record to suggest breeding status: David Easterla and Rod Leslie found a singing male and a female carrying nesting materials at Rio Grande Village on June 8, 1973.

Eastern Meadowlark

Sturnella magna

Uncommon migrant and winter visitor.

The Eastern and Western Meadowlarks are so similar that it is impossible to tell them apart without a specimen or hearing them sing. The Eastern Meadowlark's call is five or six clear whistles; that of the Western Meadowlark is loud and flutelike, the call heard in western movies. (As a child growing up in Idaho, I was told that the meadowlark said, "Salt Lake City is a pretty lit-tle city.") The Eastern Meadowlark nests throughout the open grasslands from Marathon to Fort Stockton and Alpine to Balmorhea. It has not been found to nest within the lower park of Brewster County, but it does frequent this area during the fall, winter, and spring. It apparently overwinters within the sotol grasslands and on grassy flats along the river. Road-kills examined on September 26, 1967, October 6, 1968, December 21, 1967, and January 27, 1968, from Panther Junction to the lower Tornillo Creek bridge, proved to be of this species.

It was taken on the South Rim on May 20, 1932 (Van Tyne and Sutton, 1937), and twelve to fourteen birds in a flock at the Rio Grande Village Campground in March 1967 were identified by their songs (Russ and Marian Wilson).

Western Meadowlark

Sturnella neglecta

Fairly common migrant and winter resident.

Like the eastern form, this bird can be found within the lower sotol grasslands and the grassy flats adjacent to the Rio Grande during fall, winter, and spring. It has been recorded from October 9 through May 4 but apparently does not nest in the lower Big Bend area, although Dale Zimmerman found what he believed to be a nesting bird near the K-Bar Ranch the second week of April 1971. It does nest in the higher valleys of the Davis Mountains. Road-kills found from Panther Junction to Rio Grande Village on October 15, 1967, December 2, 1967, February 1, 1969, and March 14, 1967, proved to be of this species. It can sometimes be found in quite large flocks; I found 65 or more birds near San Vicente on November 11, 1967. Harold Brodrick reported it at Panther Junction on January 17, March 9, and April 5, 1961. Several singing birds at Rio Grande Village on March 8, 1970, were of this species (Wauer).

Yellow-headed Blackbird

Xanthocephalus xanthocephalus

Fairly common migrant; rare in winter.

This large blackbird has been reported for the park every month but February and March. Spring migrants pass through the area from April 12 to May 31; they may be found singly in a flock of Brewer's Blackbirds or Brown-headed

Yellow-headed Blackbird, *Xanthocephalus xanthocephalus*

Cowbirds, or in small to large unmixed flocks. I saw 129 males at Rio Grande Village on April 25, 1969; Paul and Martha Whitson reported a mixed flock of 25 to 30 birds there on April 30, 1968; and Ty and Julie Hotchkiss saw a lone male at the top of the Lost Mine Trail (6,850 feet in elevation) on May 20, 1970. Except for one sighting of a lone bird at Grapevine Spring by James Dixon, June 14, 1956, there are no records for the park from May 31 through July 6.

Southbound birds may appear in mixed or pure flocks of males early in summer; there are several sightings of 3 to 10 males at Panther Junction on July 8 and 9, and Harold Brodrick found a flock of more than 100 birds there on July 23, 1957. I found a mixed flock of about 30 birds at Solis on July 23, 1970. There are several reports of a few to many Yellow-heads from mid-August to October 3; I observed a flock of more than 235 birds at Panther Junction on September 12 and 24, 1961. Although there are only two wintertime records for the park—Robert Tanhope observed one along the river near Black Dike on December 4, 1969, and Bruce McHenry reported one at Panther Junction on January 10, 1955—it can usually be found with flocks of blackbirds at fields and corrals throughout the northern part of the Big Bend Country all winter.

Rusty Blackbird

Euphagus carolinus

Rare fall visitor.

The first Rusty Blackbird recorded in the park was collected along an irrigation ditch at Rio Grande Village on December 10, 1967 (Wauer, 1969*b*). John Galley observed one at Hot Springs on December 27, 1967, I saw two with a flock of ten Brewer's Blackbirds and eight Brown-headed Cowbirds at Rio Grande Village on October 24, 1968, and I recorded another near the beaver pond on December 23, 1970.

Brewer's Blackbird

Euphagus cyanocephalus

Common migrant and rare winter visitor.

Spring migrants have been recorded from early March through June 7, and there is a late sighting by David Easterla of a lone male at Panther Junction on June 27, 1973; early arrivals are usually alone or in twos or threes, but by

Brewer's Blackbird, *Euphagus cyanocephalus*

April 12, flocks of 10 to 25 birds are more common. The peak of the spring migration is April 26 to May 6, and flocks of 6 to 120 (recorded at Rio Grande Village on April 28, 1967) can be found moving along the river throughout the daytime hours. Most migrants are pretty well confined to the river and lowlands, but sightings in the mountains are not uncommon. I have seen birds at a number of places in the Chisos Mountains: a lone male at the end of the Lost Mine Trail on March 21, 1967, several at the sewage lagoons on April 26, 1968, and April 26, 1969, and four flocks of 15 to 28 birds over the Basin on May 4, 1968. The Brewer's is a fairly common visitor to Panther Junction from April 12 to May 27; 7 birds were banded there from April 17 to May 1, 1970, but only 2 in the fall—on September 21, 1970, and October 3, 1969.

Fall migrants reach the park area during the first week of September, and the southward trend continues at a regular pace until late October. A few stragglers continue to pass through the area until late December. There is one January record of a lone male seen along the Black Gap road just north of the park on January 21, 1970 (Wauer). This species occurs at fields and corrals throughout the northern part of the Big Bend in winter, and Pansy Espy has found it nesting in the Davis Mountains.

Great-tailed Grackle

Quiscalus mexicanus

Uncommon along the Rio Grande in spring and rare in winter.

Most records range from the first of April through mid-June; there is one late sighting at Rio Grande Village on June 30, 1970 (Wauer). The species is present at the western edge of the park at Lajitas throughout the year. The only record of nesting is two nests found at the Rio Grande Village lake, just behind the store, on May 12, 1983, by Robert DeVine. Wintertime records include 4 birds at Santa Elena, Chihuahua, on November 19, 1967, a flock of 22 at Cottonwood Campground on December 21, 1967, and 6 there on December 30, 1968 (Wauer).

Common Grackle

Quiscalus quiscula

Five spring records (April 26–May 25), and one in fall.

It was first reported by John and Fran Nubel, Lois Schmidt, and Ruth Carter at Panther Junction on May 12, 1968. It was next recorded by James Clarke, who observed one male Common Grackle in a flock of "Boat-tailed Grackles" at Castolon on April 26, 1975. There were three 1978 sightings: one male at Panther Junction on May 13 (park files); one there on May 20 (Karen Bennack and A. J. Revels); and one at a feeder there on November 27 and 28 (Robert DeVine and Jimmie Stovall). And Jacob Miller reported one at the Basin Campground on May 24 and 25, 1980.

Bronzed Cowbird

Molothrus aeneus

Local summer visitor only since 1969.

On June 9, 1969, David Easterla found four males and two females at Rio Grande Village. One of the males was courting the females; it was last seen on July 4 (Wauer). The species was again recorded on June 8, 1970 (Easterla), and at least six males and four females stayed in the Rio Grande Village Campground area until July 3. On July 12 I found, hanging on a tamarisk near the Daniels house, a Hooded Oriole nest that contained two juvenile Bronzed Cowbirds (one was collected). On July 18 the nest was empty and a juvenile Bronzed Cowbird was found 55 feet away being fed by both adult

Hooded Orioles. On July 28 I discovered another young Bronzed Cowbird at an Orchard Oriole nest near the large pond; Easterla and I watched the youngster being fed by the adult female Orchard Oriole on July 30.

In 1971, an adult male appeared at Panther Junction on May 22 and remained until May 29, when it was banded and released; it did not return. I found four males and four females at Rio Grande Village on May 29, and at least a few of these individuals remained through July 13; a juvenile Bronzed Cowbird was seen begging from an Orchard Oriole on August 4. Also in 1971, I found the species present at Cottonwood Campground from June 5 through July 10.

It appears that this species is increasing within the Big Bend area and will probably become a regular breeding bird, as it is in the lower Rio Grande Valley. If this is the case, it is likely that the populations of breeding Orchard and Hooded Orioles along the floodplain will decrease.

Brown-headed Cowbird

Molothrus ater

Abundant summer resident along the floodplain, at Panther Junction, and in the Chisos Basin, and less numerous elsewhere below 5,500 feet; common migrant and rare winter visitor.

Breeding birds belong to the small *obscurus* race of cowbirds that is sometimes referred to as the Dwarf Cowbird. They arrive on their breeding grounds during the first and second weeks of April and parasitize a great number of the park's smaller nesting species, including the Black-tailed Gnatcatcher, Bell's Vireo, Yellow-breasted Chat, House Sparrow, Blue Grosbeak, Painted Bunting, and Black-throated Sparrow. All breeding birds above 2,500 feet in elevation in the Chisos Mountains may be one huge flock;

birds banded at Panther Junction have been regularly recorded in the Basin. Adult Dwarf Cowbirds move out of their breeding grounds the last week of July but are replaced immediately by a larger race (*artemisae*) during the first week of August. Some local youngsters intermingle with the larger birds, which may remain until early September. By mid-September only an occasional migrant is to be found.

Spring migrants have been recorded along the river and in the lowlands from March 17 to early June. Early arrivals are usually alone or in small flocks, but many larger flocks can be found when the main movement gets under way, from the first of April to mid-May. Northbound birds are most numerous in the lowlands but occasionally are seen at Laguna Meadow, Boot Canyon, and the South Rim in late May and early June. Fall migrants have not been recorded above 5,500 feet. Flocks of three to thirty birds occur regularly to mid-September, and a few stragglers have been recorded until October 24. There are no November records, but a rare winter visitor was seen at Panther Junction in late December and January. Brown-headed Cowbirds winter with Brewer's Blackbirds throughout the northern Big Bend Country.

Black-vented Oriole

Icterus wagleri

One series of sightings.

A single adult female was regularly seen at Rio Grande Village between mid-April and early October in 1969 and 1970 (Wauer, 1970*b*). It was first discovered on September 27, 1968; I watched it for several minutes among the foliage of the thicket of vegetation along the nature trail. I later compared the black crissum and other characteristics to oriole identities in Blake (1953) and Sutton (1951) and was able to identify the bird without doubt as Wagler's Oriole, or Black-vented Oriole, the name preferred by the

American Ornithologists' Union. I could not find it the following morning.

On April 28, 1969, I again saw an adult Wagler's less than three hundred feet from the first sighting. For more than forty minutes I watched it and six other orioles (an adult female and an immature male Hooded Oriole, and two female, one adult, and one immature male Orchard Oriole) chase each other from tree to tree within the Rio Grande Village Campground. The Wagler's Oriole appeared to be in close association with the immature male Hooded Oriole, which nicely fit Sutton's description of a female Wagler. Although I have since learned that the species is monomorphic (having a single color pattern), I assumed that this was a possible nesting pair.

On May 1, as I was again observing the Wagler's Oriole at the same location (with, presumably, the same six orioles), I met Ty and Julie Hotchkiss, who were camped at Rio Grande Village. When I informed them of the bird's identity, they graciously offered to photograph the bird for further documentation. During the following three weeks, they took more than fifty feet of 16mm movie film and eight color slides. *I. wagleri* was further authenticated by the observation of the following people: Mr. and Mrs. H. T. Hargis (they also obtained excellent photographs), Terry Hall, Kay McCracken, Doris Maguire, Russ and Marian Wilson, Doyle and Helen Peckham, Warren and Bobby Pulich, Charles and Betty Crabtree, David Wolf, Jim Tucker, Doug Eddleman, and Mike Parmeter in May; David Easterla, Guy McCaskie, Cliff Lyons, and Ginger Coughran in June; and Bob Smith and Paul Sykes in July.

These data represent the first authenticated records of the Wagler's Oriole for the United States, although there is a questionable sighting by Herbert Brown from the Patagonia Mountains of Arizona in 1910 (Phillips, 1968). South of the border, it occurs "from Sonora, Chihuahua, and Nuevo León, south through Guatemala and Honduras to El Salvador (in winter) and northern Nicaragua" (Freidmann, Griscom, and Moore, 1957). The Mexican breeding records nearest to Big Bend National Park are from 15 miles south of Gómez Farias, in the state of Coahuila, where Charles Ely (1962) studied the avifauna in the southeastern part of the state. Gómez Farias is 350 miles from the Big Bend.

By mid-May it was evident that the Wagler's Oriole at Rio Grande Village was not nesting, and that we had only a single bird. Its behavior gave no indication that it was defending a territory. Yet by midmorning it would usually disappear into the dense floodplain vegetation and often did not return to the campground portion of its range until late afternoon or evening. By 6:30 a.m. it was always back in the campground with many immature Orchards or the one or two immature Hooded Orioles that were still present. All these seemed to prefer the fruits of the squaw-bush, which were ripening throughout May and June. On May 19 I watched *I. wagleri* feed on flowers of desert willow for several minutes, and on June 28 it caught a cicada, tore the wings off, and consumed the softer parts of the body, dropping the rest to the ground.

In order to obtain close-up photographs for the racial identification, as well as to band the bird so that it would be recognized if it returned again, I made several attempts to net it between June 28 and July 4. On July 1, I placed a mounted Great Horned Owl, a species that occurs commonly in the immediate vicinity, on the ground next to a mist net. *I. wagleri* perched ten feet above the stuffed bird and watched while a pair of Northern Mockingbirds launched attack after attack on the owl until both were caught in the netting. I even drew a Wagler's Oriole on paper, colored it with the proper colors, and mounted the drawing on a stick next to the net. This, too, was a failure—*I. wagleri*'s only reaction was one of vague curiosity.

Yet it did show interest in people on a number of occasions. Several times I observed it watching campers going about their routine duties, and on one occasion it flew into a tree above two children who were rolling a red rubber ball around on the ground. It sat there watching this action for about four minutes before flying off to another perch. On only two occasions did I observe it showing any aggression toward another bird, and then only two very short chases (fifteen to twenty feet) of female Orchard Orioles. Although *I. wagleri* could usually be detected by the very low, rasping call it gave, like that of a Yellow-breasted Chat or a Scott's Oriole, a song was never heard.

Finally, by moving the nets each time *I. wagleri* changed positions, I succeeded in capturing it on July 4. Closer examination showed that it was in nonbreeding status; it clearly lacked evidence of a brood patch and had no cloacal protuberance. Close examination of the bill and cere showed no indication that the bird had been caged at any time. Close-up photographs of the chest were sent to Allan Phillips, who identified the bird racially as the *wagleri* form of eastern Mexico. The chest had a light chestnut tinge.

After carefully photographing the major features of the bird, I placed a band (no. 632–25253) on its right leg and released it. It immediately flew south to the floodplain portion of the range, dived into the dense vegetation, and was not seen the rest of the day. By July 10, however, it was right back in the same habits and allowed good binocular examination for the first half of each morning.

In early August it became quite shy and had to be searched for among the dense foliage along the nature trail. I last saw it that year on September 19, exactly one year after the original date of discovery. In 1970, I found it again in the same locality from April 17 through September 21 and again on October 10. A goodly number of birders observed the same banded bird throughout the summer, but it has not been seen since.

Orchard Oriole

Icterus spurius

Abundant summer resident (April 11–September 28) at Rio Grande Village but less common along the rest of the floodplain.

This is a very gregarious species, and the birds spend the early part of the breeding season chasing one another around their territories. Only males are known to sing; second-year males sing and nest as well. Nesting occurs during May, June, and July, although I found an adult Orchard Oriole feeding a young Bronzed Cowbird on July 28, 1970.

There is considerable postnesting wandering, particularly among immature birds, and they may be found to 4,500 feet. One was seen along the lower part of the Window Trail on July 9, 1962, and they are regular at Panther Junction and adjacent washes from late July to early September. Females and immature birds were banded at Panther Junction on July 21, 1970, August 6 and 20, 1967, September 7,

Orchard Oriole, *Icterus spurius*

1967, and September 20, 1969. By early September this bird becomes rare on its breeding grounds; I have seen only one adult male later than the first of September, although adult females and immatures can usually be found with some effort. There is one wintertime sighting: M. S. Croft reported a lone male at Rio Grande Village on December 24, 1980.

Hooded Oriole

Icterus cucullatus

Fairly common summer resident at Rio Grande Village and the adjacent floodplain but less common elsewhere along the river; rare migrant.

It has been recorded from March 16 through October 1. Adult males arrive on their breeding grounds from the last of March to the first of April, and it is several days before females and subadults put in their appearance. Like the Orchard Oriole, Hooded Orioles are very gregarious at first and can often be found chasing other Hooded Orioles and Orchard Orioles. Nest-building begins by mid-May; the earliest nest-building I have found was at Rio Grande Village on May 11, 1970. Young are fledged in June and July: adults were found feeding nestlings on May 24, 1969; two fledged birds were seen at Rio Grande Village on July 17, 1968; and a nest containing two young Bronzed Cowbirds was discovered there in a tamarisk on July 12, 1970 (Wauer). Apparently there is also some late nesting: I found a new nest under construction near the top of a tall cottonwood at Rio Grande Village on July 18, 1970.

Postnesting birds do not seem to wander as much as Orchard Orioles, although there appears to be some movement into the mountains; I found an adult male feeding at a century plant near the Basin Campground on August 1, 1966, and one female at Juniper Flat on August 10, 1969. Migrants have been recorded on only a few occasions. It is assumed that early birds in mid-March are migrants; I found adult males at Panther Junction on March 19, 1967, and April 17, 1970. Fall migrants are rare in the mountains; I found one in the Basin on October 1, 1966.

Northern Oriole

Icterus galbula

This is another case of two identifiable birds being lumped into one species by the revised AOU *Check-list* (1983). Since these two can be distinguished in the field, I will discuss them separately here.

Baltimore Oriole

Three sightings in the park.

Dixon and Wallmo (1956) first collected one at Black Gap Wildlife Management Area on June 20, 1955; Bobbie Pettit and Ruth and Harvey Williams observed a male at Rio Grande Village on April 29, 1978; and Vermille Ruff reported a male at Castolon on May 21, 1979.

Bullock's Oriole

Uncommon migrant (early April–mid-May, mid-August–mid-September).

There are also some summer records: Tarleton Smith found one at Boquillas on June 21, 1936, and Jim Scudday collected an adult male along Alamito Creek, seventeen miles southeast of Marfa, on June 10, 1968. The majority of the park sightings are of lone birds, but five (two adult males and three females or immatures) were found on the Rio Grande Village Nature Trail on August 20 and 22, 1970 (Wauer). Although the majority of records are from the lowlands, there is one from Boot Spring on April 12, 1956 (Harold Brodrick), one from Laguna Meadow on May 6, 1968 (Ned Fritz), one from the Chisos Basin on August 31, 1967, and one from Lost Mine Trail on September 19, 1967 (Wauer). There is no evidence of nesting within the park, nor has Pansy Espy found it nesting in the Davis Mountains. It is a common summer resident in the El Paso area and eastward along the Rio Grande (McBee and Keefer, 1967).

Scott's Oriole

Icterus parisorum

Common summer resident of the yucca-sotol grasslands; common migrant.

The Scott's Oriole usually remains in the park until the first severe cold front reaches the Big Bend. It has been recorded every month of the year. Adult males arrive first in spring; singing males were recorded in lower Green Gulch on March 19, 1969, and at the Basin on April 17, 1968 (Wauer). Females and subadults arrive a few days later, and nesting begins immediately rather than being preceded by a period of play, as is the case with the Orchard and Hooded Orioles. Nesting has been recorded at Panther Junction as early as March 23, 1960 (Harold Brodrick); Van Tyne and Sutton (1937) reported young already out of the nest at Boquillas on May 16, 1933. I found a nest on a Torrey yucca near Santa Elena Canyon on April 28, 1968, and banded three nestlings at the Basin on June 8, 1970. This last nest was located on a beaked yucca in front of the motel unit. Another nest was built within a few inches of the first one and young were seen on August 9; I assumed that it belonged to the same adults.

The postnesting period appears to be the main time for play for this oriole, and there is some flocking; a flock of fifteen birds (five adults and ten immatures) was seen along the Window Trail on September 10, 1967 (Wauer).

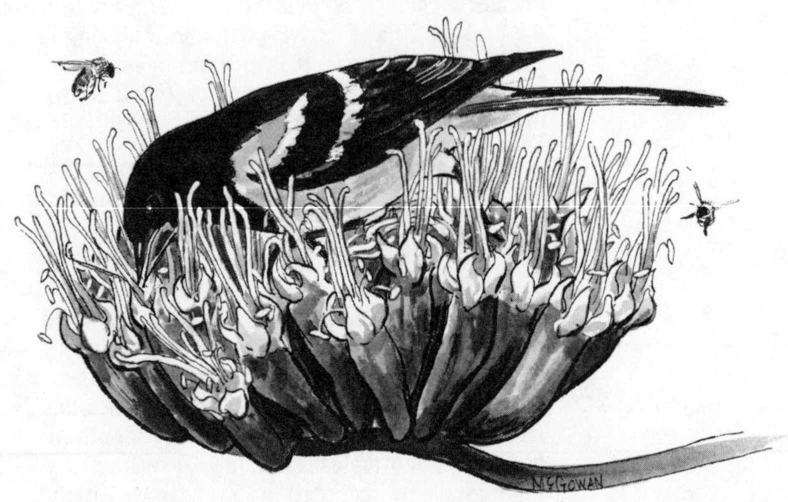

Scott's Oriole, *Icterus parisorum*

Family groups of three to seven birds are more common and are sometimes found considerably above their nesting grounds. I recorded lone birds at Laguna Meadow (6,300 feet in elevation) on September 4, 1967, and September 8, 1969, and an adult male and two females at 6,850 feet at the end of the Lost Mine Trail on October 24, 1968. Some birds remain on their breeding grounds throughout the fall and early winter. Seven individuals were seen along Oak Creek just below the Basin Campground on December 1, 1968, and three were found there on December 23. Apparently, it may even stay throughout the winter; I found an immature male on the open mesquite flats near Boquillas Canyon on December 29, 1970, and January 16, 1971.

Finches:
Family Fringillidae

Purple Finch

Carpodacus purpureus

Four park records.

This species was first reported on April 13, 1972, by P. Phillips and J. Greenberg, who observed two singing males and one female at Rio Grande Village. On May 13, 1975, they again found two males and one female, at the Old Sam Nail Ranch. And Mr. and Mrs. H. E. Poindexter reported one at Rio Grande Village on August 26, 1975. Rick LoBello found one female, which he observed from fifteen feet, at Panther Junction on December 20, 1976.

Cassin's Finch

Carpodacus cassinii

Irregular visitor to the Chisos highlands any time of year.

Cassin's Finch has been recorded every month but September, but it seems to be somewhat sporadic in occurrence. It was seen several times in 1966–67: I found one in the Basin on August 13; Leon Bishop reported a "flock of about one dozen" in the pines on the Lost Mine Trail on October 20; and I found two there on November 6, two more at the South Rim on January 29, one at Boot Spring on March 30, one flying over the Basin on April 2 and 6, and one at Boot Spring on June 8. It was not reported again until July 20, 1969, when I found a lone male near Laguna Meadow. Tony Gallucci reported a pair on the Window Trail on May 16, 1975, and Wesley Cureton found four females at Laguna Meadow on December 29, 1977.

House Finch

Carpodacus mexicanus

Common resident below 5,500 feet; common spring migrant.

At least a few can be found almost any place below 5,500 feet at any time of the year. Nesting begins early on the desert and fledged birds can be found by late April or early May. During wet years this species may nest in July and August as well. Of special interest was a nest built in an abandoned Cliff Swallow nest at Hot Springs on March 29, 1968. Postnesting birds occasionally wander into the higher canyons, such as Boot Canyon, where I found it on August 10, 1968, but for the most part, the species is restricted to lower areas. Family groups become the nucleus of flocks that may number 50 to 150 birds during fall, winter, and spring. There is a considerable increase in House Finches during a brief period from mid-March through mid-April.

Red Crossbill

Loxia curvirostra

Sporadic visitor to the Chisos woodlands.

This highland species was first reported for the Chisos Mountains by Oberholser (1902), who found it there in June 1901 and considered it to be a probable breeding species. Although it may nest during wet years or invasion years, I found no evidence of nesting from 1966 to 1972. One or two sightings are reported almost every year, and some years this species is common. The winter of 1967–68 was apparently an invasion year, because the Red Crossbill was abundant in the Chisos from August 13 through June 11. I found twelve birds foraging on piñons at Laguna Meadow on November 15, four along the East Rim on January 28, twelve near the Pinnacles on May 3, and forty near Boot Spring

House Finch, *Carpodacus mexicanus*

on May 25. A specimen taken on May 3 represents the *benti* race that breeds in the Rocky Mountains from northern New Mexico to Utah and Montana.

Pine Siskin

Carduelis pinus

Fairly common migrant; uncommon winter visitor; a few summertime sightings.

It has been reported every month but July. The earliest fall sightings are for the Chisos Basin during the last half of August; David Easterla found one there on August 16, 1973, and David Wolf reported a flock of seventeen on August 19, 1968. It is rare in September (I found one at Rio Grande Village on September 19, 1969) and during the first two months of October. Afterward, it becomes more numerous until mid-November, and there is a gradual shifting of sightings from the mountains into the lowlands. In spring it is most common from mid-March through May 20. Although large flocks of Pine Siskins may remain through mid-May, only stragglers are to be expected thereafter. There are no indications of nesting within the park, although Charles Bender found it nesting at Madera Park in the Davis Mountains on June 6, 1970.

Lesser Goldfinch

Carduelis psaltria

Fairly common summer and winter resident.

This is the common goldfinch of the Big Bend area. Although it can usually be found in the mountains and along the river any time of the year, it is most numerous in the mountains in summer and along the river in winter. Nesting occurs from May through September. It prefers

Lesser Goldfinch, *Carduelis psaltria*

areas of broadleaf trees and shrubs but can be found on conifers as well. I have found singing males among the Arizona cypress in Boot Canyon during the second week of August in 1968 and 1969. Gerry Wolfe reported a nest with two young on a cypress tree next to the Boot Spring cabin on September 16, 1982.

American Goldfinch

Carduelis tristis

Fairly common spring migrant; uncommon in fall and winter.

It has been recorded every month but June and July. The earliest fall record is one collected at Oak Creek on September 8, 1956 (Texas A&M), but it does not occur regularly until the last of October, after which a few individuals can usually be found along the river and in the mountain canyons throughout the winter. Flocks of fifteen to thirty birds are most common, but a flock of sixty was found at Boot Canyon on November 4, 1967 (Wauer). Spring migrants begin to move into the area during the second week of March, and they become fairly common until mid-April. Sightings lapse for a couple of weeks, then become numerous again from the last of April to May 25. There is also a single June sighting of three birds in the Basin on June 10, 1968 (Wauer).

Evening Grosbeak

Coccothraustes vespertinus

Four park records.

Karl Haller first reported this species in the Chisos Basin on the 1951 Christmas Count (December 30). Mr. and Mrs. Don Troyer found it "between the Basin Trailhead and Boulder Meadow" on November 13, 1972. Jack Tyler reported one female at Boot Spring on May 20, 1974, and Bonnie McKinney reported six males at the Chisos Remuda on October 31, 1983.

Old World Sparrows: *Family Passeridae*

House Sparrow

Passer domesticus

Common resident at areas of human habitation: Rio Grande Village, Castolon, Panther Junction, and the Chisos Basin.

Van Tyne and Sutton (1937) reported one taken at Glenn Spring on July 26, 1928, that represents the first for the park area. It is of some interest that this species no longer resides at Glenn Spring, probably because of the present lack of human occupation there. This may be one of the few instances on record when the House Sparrow deserted an area; records are usually of invasions. Tarleton Smith reported in 1936 that although the species was present at Boquillas and settlements along the Rio Grande, "none have found our camp in the Basin." The area of the Basin Campground, Remuda, and Lodge is now one of the House Sparrow strongholds. In 1963, C. Philip Allen reported that he found only "4 pairs" of House Sparrows at Panther Junction. A conservative estimate of the 1970 population there exceeded two hundred birds. It is impossible to estimate how long the species has been in the Big Bend area, but Montgomery (1905) reported it as common at Alpine as early as June 1904.

House Sparrows in the park seem to be quite mobile. Birds banded at Panther Junction also frequent the Basin Remuda. Rio Grande Village House Sparrows spend most of their time there in winter and spring but are most numerous at Boquillas, Coahuila, during summer and fall.

Birds of Uncertain Occurrence

The following birds are not contained within the regular annotated list because they need further documentation. In general, this hypothetical list includes those species that have not been authenticated by either a specimen or a sighting by more than two or three individuals or parties.

Anhinga

Anhinga anhinga

Wildlife photographer Bert Schaughency and his wife, Millie, saw one flying over the river at Hot Springs on April 23, 1970. As far as can be determined, this is the westernmost sighting in Texas; there is one 1886 record for Pecos County.

Red-breasted Merganser

Mergus serrator

Samuel Fried reported seeing a lone female at Hot Springs on May 1, 1977. This species has been reported at Lake Balmorhea on a number of occasions.

Masked Duck

Oxyura dominica

There are two sightings of this little Mexican duck in the park. A pair was first reported in Santa Elena Canyon by Bill Mealy, Dave Mobley, and Michael Allender on March 29, 1978. And on April 11, 1978, C. E. Hall reported three females at Hot Springs.

Northern Bobwhite

Colinus virginianus

Chuck Sexton reported flushing a male bobwhite and hearing two additional birds singing their "covey call" at Rio Grande Village on August 3, 1982. Bonnie McKinney informed me that J. P. Bryan, owner of Chalk Draw Ranch (west of Persimmon Gap), has introduced this species to his ranch in recent years.

Black Rail

Laterallus jamaicensis

Verma Starts reported that she identified this bird from a "close look" at Rio Grande Village on March 5, 1978. The nearest sightings of this bird in Texas are from the Gulf Coast.

Spotted Rail

Pardirallus maculatus

Jody Miller reported seeing this Mexican rail on the Boquillas Canyon Nature Trail in February 1978. The AOU *Check-list* (1983) includes two previous records for the United States: in Brownwood, Texas, and Beaver County, Pennsylvania.

Whooping Crane

Grus americana

Jim Liles reported three whoopers flying over Rio Grande Village on the morning of October 23, 1982; they circled three times before flying eastward toward Boquillas Canyon.

Mountain Plover

Charadrius montanus

This grassland migrant is included here because of a report of a lone bird at a stock tank at the south end of Black Gap Wildlife Management Area, on August 27, 1982, by Bonnie McKinney.

Red Knot

Calidris canutus

There is a single record of this bird for the park area: I observed one at a pond at Rio Grande Village on September 3, 1966.

Pectoral Sandpiper

Calidris melanotos

The only park record of this shorebird is one reported by Lovie Mae Whitaker for Hot Springs on July 19, 1942.

Stilt Sandpiper

Calidris himantopus

Bonnie McKinney reported this bird at a stock tank at Black Gap Wildlife Management Area on September 29, 1981.

Buff-breasted Sandpiper

Tryngites subruficollis

This grassland peep was reported by Bonnie McKinney at Black Gap Wildlife Management Area headquarters, August 24, 1982. She said that it was also seen by the Parks and Wildlife biologist.

Common Tern

Sterna hirundo

A lone bird was reported twice in May 1978. It was first seen at the Lajitas Cavalry Post by Craig McIntyre on May 5; Jeanne Farmer reported one at Rio Grande Village on May 9.

Black Tern

Chlidonias niger

There are no park records of this tern, but it appears to be a rare spring and fall visitor at water areas throughout the Big Bend. Clay and Jody Miller recorded it on their ranch, near Valentine, on August 23, 1956, May 20, 1957, and August 30, 1965; I observed one just west of Marathon on August 21, 1970; and Jim Scudday collected one of several seen at Lake Balmorhea on September 16, 1970.

Red-billed Pigeon

Columba flavirostris

There are two unconfirmed sightings of this southern pigeon. Alexander Sprunt, Jr., and

John H. Dick reported seeing two fly over their cottages in the Chisos Basin on July 21, 1951. It was seen "in good light and at low elevation, which revealed characteristics perfectly." It was reported again at the Panther Junction housing area by Pete Peterson, July 19, 1981.

Black-billed Cuckoo

Coccyzus erythropthalmus

I found a lone cuckoo among the oaks in Boot Canyon on June 16, 1976, that I believe was this species. And Gordon Kennedy reported an immature bird in Boot Canyon on October 14, 1979.

Squirrel Cuckoo

Piaya cayana

J. T. Ramirez reported two of these southern cuckoos in the Rio Grande Village Campground on June 13, 1980.

Ferruginous Pygmy-Owl

Glaucidium brasilianum

This little owl has been reported twice: Steve Berg found one ten miles north of Marathon on May 31, 1977; and Ada Foster reported it at Rio Grande Village on April 11, 1980.

Spotted Owl

Strix occidentalis

Bonnie McKinney reported two observations at Black Gap Wildlife Management Area along Farm Road 2627 on June 25 and 30, 1982.

Barred Owl

Strix varia

Mr. and Mrs. Robert Foster reported hearing this eastern owl calling several times within Reagan Canyon, below La Linda on the Rio Grande, during the night of November 25, 1971. And Mr. and Mrs. H. E. Poindexter reported one sitting in the roadway in Green Gulch during the evening of August 27, 1975.

Black Swift

Cypseloides niger

There are two reports of this western swift for the park: Alexander Sprunt, Jr., and John H. Dick reported "five or six individuals" from the South Rim Trail over Blue Creek Canyon on July 22, 1951; and Fran Nubel and Ruth Carter reported one at Santa Elena Canyon on May 9, 1968.

White-necked Jacobin

Florisuga mellivora

Doris and Russ Phipps and Shirley and Arch Sink reported a large hummingbird that they identified as this large species at the beaver pond on the Rio Grande Village Nature Trail, May 6 and 7, 1979.

Ringed Kingfisher

Ceryle torquata

There are two sightings of this large kingfisher reported within the park: Bill Mealy and Dave

Mobley found one in Santa Elena Canyon on March 29, 1978; and Robert DeVine and Ted, Bob, and Karen Jones reported one at Hot Springs on July 28, 1981.

Downy Woodpecker

Picoides pubescens

Doyle and Helen Peckham reported seeing this little woodpecker at Rio Grande Village Campground on May 17, 1969.

Hairy Woodpecker

Picoides villosus

Brodrick (1960) included this bird in his park listing on the basis of a reported sighting at an unknown place in the park for March 10, 1950. T. Paul Bonney reported one female at Rio Grande Village Campground, May 12, 1973. And there is a record of one at Black Gap Wildlife Management Area headquarters on April 13, 1983 (Bonnie McKinney).

Three-toed Woodpecker

Picoides tridactylus

William North reported this species at Panther Junction on May 15, 1983.

Northern Beardless-Tyrannulet

Camptostoma imberbe

Len Robinson and Eleanor Beal reported this

little flycatcher at two locations on April 2, 1975: Green Gulch and the Window Trail.

Buff-breasted Flycatcher

Empidonax fulvifrons

This little flycatcher was reported from near the Chisos Remuda in the Basin by Dr. and Mrs. R. C. Smith, August 12, 1969.

Great Kiskadee

Pitangus sulphuratus

There are three reports: Roy and Jean Hudson reported one along the river at Boquillas on May 21, 1964; N. Dobbins reported one at Rio Grande Village on December 30, 1979; and Pierce reported one male near the beginning of the Santa Elena Canyon Nature Trail on May 18, 1983.

Pinyon Jay

Gymnorhinus cyanocephalus

Sheriton Burr reported seeing a lone Pinyon Jay with a flock of Gray-breasted Jays on the Lost Mine Trail, May 5, 1978.

Black-billed Magpie

Pica pica

Phil and Charlotte Spencer reported that a magpie flew across the road near the Old Sam Nail Ranch on February 15, 1981.

American Crow

Corvus brachyrhynchos

Barbara Ribble reported seeing two crows fly over Castolon on December 27, 1970.

Chickadee

Parus sps.

There are two reports within the park: Bernard Browerhand first reported seeing five or six chickadees that sang a "coarse chickadee call" in Boot Canyon on June 26, 1974; Mr. and Mrs. F. P. Elby reported six to twelve "very noisy chickadees" on the Lost Mine Trail on August 21, 1975.

Bridled Titmouse

Parus wollweberi

Mr. and Mrs. Edward Dickman first reported one at Hot Springs on May 1, 1975. Steve Berg reported one with several Black-throated Sparrows at Panther Junction on September 1, 1975. Henry West and M. E. Gibson found five individuals with a flock of Bushtits in the Chisos Basin on May 12, 1981. Bonnie McKinney reported two on the Window Trail, November 16, 1981.

American Dipper

Cinclus mexicanus

Steve Zachary and Jim Walker reported one on upper Fresno Creek, February 25, 1975, that "flew from under a waterfall—landed on a rock—bobbed up and down." Bonnie McKinney reported one at a creek just east of the Agua Fria Ranch headquarters, 65 miles south of Alpine, on November 12, 1980.

Clay-colored Robin

Turdus grayi

Mr. and Mrs. R. N. Hewitt reported finding one with several American Robins at Rio Grande Village on March 6, 1977.

Bohemian Waxwing

Bombycilla garrulus

R. C. Frankenberger and G. Winington reported a waxwing with "white in the wings" that they identified as a Bohemian at Rio Grande Village, May 8, 1975.

Tropical Parula

Parula pitiayumi

I found a lone bird in heavy vegetation at the Boquillas Ranger Station on March 19, 1967, that I believed to be of this species. Joanne Kangas reported one in Santa Elena Canyon on March 23, 1967. Scott Carroll and Fred Harris reported one on the Window Trail on March 22, 1976. And Robert Harms reported one with several Yellow-rumped Warblers (Audubon's race) at Rio Grande Village, January 3, 1979.

Pine Warbler

Dendroica pinus

David T. Brown and members of the San Antonio Audubon Society reported seeing this bird at Boot Spring on April 27, 1966.

Cerulean Warbler

Dendroica cerulea

Bonnie McKinney reported finding three individuals in brush around a stock tank at Black Gap Wildlife Management Area on March 29, 1982.

Slate-throated Redstart

Myioborus miniatus

V. Lee Grover reported finding this species at Rio Grande Village on July 4, 1976; he reported it "had no white in the wings." John H. Bronaugh reported one from the same locality on May 20, 1980.

Golden-crowned Warbler

Basileuterus culicivorus

Bill Mealy reported finding a lone bird of this species at Laguna Meadow on April 18, 1982.

Olive Sparrow

Arremonops rufivirgatus

Scott Robinson reported one at the Old Sam Nail Ranch on April 30, 1976.

Blue-black Grassquit

Volatinia jacarina

Bonnie McKinney reported this species at Black Gap Wildlife Management Area, just north of the park, on the following occasions: a flock of sixteen females during the last two weeks of August 1982; one male on September 2, 1982; one male and one female on November 26, 1982.

Yellow-eyed Junco

Junco phaeonotus

There is an old undated record in the park files for along the Window Trail, and the species was reported twice in 1980: Mr. and Mrs. W. L. Erwin found ten to fifteen at Boot Spring on April 3, and P. J. Paicich and R. S. Naveen reported one there on June 17. This is a common breeding bird in the Maderas del Carmen range of Mexico, fifty miles to the southeast, and postnesting visitors should be expected.

McCown's Longspur

Calcarius mccownii

Steve Johnson and Nancy Saulsbury reported two birds at the K-Bar Ranch on March 8, 1981; and Bonnie McKinney reported one at Black Gap Wildlife Management Area headquarters on January 13, 1982.

Altamira Oriole

Icterus gularis

Bonnie McKinney reported this bird at Black

Gap Wildlife Management Area headquarters throughout the day of March 29, 1982, and Kathleen Stewart reported a pair at Rio Grande Village on October 12, 1982.

Audubon's Oriole

Icterus graduacauda

This bird was called the Black-headed Oriole until the publication of the 1983 AOU *Check-list*. There have been persistent reports of this species within the park for many years; all that I have checked out have been Scott's Orioles.

Pine Grosbeak

Pinicola enucleator

Clara and Harold Spore reported seeing one of this northern species in Green Gulch on April 24, 1951, and Jane Hamilton reported one at Rio Grande Village on May 5, 1982.

Lawrence's Goldfinch

Carduelis lawrencei

Doug Bernard reported one at the Chisos Basin residences on March 26, 1977.

Hooded Grosbeak

Hesperiphona abeillie

V. Lee Grover reported this species in upper Green Gulch on July 30, 1982.

Bibliography

Allen, T. M. 1977. A Survey of the Avifaunal Associates of *Agave havardiana trel.* in Big Bend National Park. M.A. thesis, University of Texas at Arlington.

———, and R. L. Neill. 1979. Avifaunal Associates of *Agave havardiana trel.* in Big Bend National Park. In: *Proceedings of the First Conference on Scientific Research in the National Parks, Vol. 1.* U.S. Department of the Interior, National Park Service, Transactions and Proceedings Series, no. 5:479–482.

American Ornithologists' Union. 1983. *Check-list of North American Birds,* 6th ed. Lawrence, KS: Allen Press, Inc.

Arnold, Keith A. 1968. Olivaceous Flycatcher in the Davis Mountains of Texas. *Bulletin of the Texas Ornithological Society* 2:28.

Bailey, Vernon. 1905. Biological Survey of Texas. *North American Fauna,* no. 25. Washington, DC.

Baker, James K. 1962. Association of Cave Swallows with Cliff and Barn Swallows. *Condor* 64:326.

Barlow, Jon C. 1967. Nesting of the Black-capped Vireo in the Chisos Mountains, Texas. *Condor* 69:605–606.

———. 1977. Effects of Habitat Attrition on Vireo Distribution and Population Density in the Northern Chihuahuan Desert. In: *Transactions of the Symposium on the Biological Resources of the Chihuahuan Desert Region, U.S. and Mexico.* U.S. Department of the Interior, National Park Service, Transactions and Proceedings Series, no. 3:591–596.

———, and R. Roy Johnson. 1967. Current Status of the Elf Owl in the Southwestern United States. *Southwestern Naturalist* 12:331–332.

———, and Roland H. Wauer. 1971. The Gray Vireo (*Vireo vicinior* Coues; Aves: Vireonidae) Wintering in the Big Bend Region, West Texas. *Canadian Journal of Zoology* 49:953–955.

Blair, W. Frank. 1950. The Biotic Provinces of Texas. *Texas Journal of Science* 2:93–116.

Blake, Emmet R. 1953. *Birds of Mexico.* Chicago: University of Chicago Press.

Borell, Adrey E. 1938. New Bird Records for Brewster County, Texas. *Condor* 40:181–182.

———. 1963. Birds Observed in the Big Bend Area of Brewster County, Texas. Typewritten report to National Park Service.

Brandt, Herbert W. 1928. Two New Birds from the Chisos Mountains, Texas. *Auk* 55:269–270.

———. 1940. *Texas Bird Adventures*. Cleveland: Bird Research Foundation.

Brodkorb, Pierce. 1935. A New Flycatcher from Texas. Occasional Papers, Museum of Zoology, University of Michigan, no. 306.

Brodrick, Harold. 1960. Check-list of the Birds of Big Bend National Park. Mimeographed. Big Bend National Park, TX.

———, C. Philip Allen, and Anne LeSassier. 1966. *Check-list of Birds of Big Bend National Park*. Big Bend National Park, TX: Big Bend Natural History Association.

Brownlee, W. C. 1977. Nesting Peregrine Falcons in Texas. Texas Parks and Wildlife Department report, no. W-103-R-071.

Correll, Donovan S., and Marshall C. Johnston. 1970. *Manual of Vascular Plants of Texas*. Renner, Texas: Texas Research Foundation.

Cottam, Clarence, and J. B. Trefenthen, eds. 1968. *Whitewings: The Life History, Status, and Management of the Whitewing Dove*. New York: D. Van Nostrand Co.

Cruickshank, Allen. 1950. Records from Brewster County, Texas. *Wilson Bulletin* 62:217–219.

Dixon, Keith L. 1959. Ecological and Distributional Relations of Desert Scrub Birds of Western Texas. *Condor* 61:397–409.

———, and O. C. Wallmo. 1965. Some New Bird Records from Brewster County, Texas. *Condor* 58:166.

Ely, Charles A. 1962. The Birds of Southeastern Coahuila, Mexico. *Condor* 64:34–39.

Espy, Pansy. 1969. Birds of the Davis Mountains. *The Phalarope*, September. Mimeographed by Midland Naturalists, Midland, Texas.

Fox, R. P. 1954. Plumages and Territorial Behavior of the Lucifer Hummingbird in the Chisos Mountains, Texas. *Auk* 71:465–466.

Freidmann, Herbert, L. Griscom, and R. T. Moore. 1957. Distributional Check-list of the Birds of Mexico, Part II. *Pacific Coast Avifauna* 33:1–435.

Fuertes, Louis Agassiz. 1903. With the Mearn's Quail in Southwestern Texas. *Condor* 5:113–116.

Galley, John E. 1951. Clark's Nutcracker in the Chisos Mountains, Texas. *Wilson Bulletin* 62:188.

Gallucci, Tony. 1978. The Biological and Taxonomic Status of the White-winged Doves of the Big Bend of Texas. M.S. thesis, Sul Ross State University, Alpine, TX.

Gehlbach, F. R. 1967. New Records of Warblers in Texas. *Southwestern Naturalist* 12:109–110.

Hill, K. B., and L. J. Schaetzel. 1977. Peregrine Falcons in Big Bend National Park: 1977 Breeding Season. Typewritten report to National Park Service by Chihuahuan Desert Research Institute.

Hitchcock, Mark A. 1977. A Survey of the Peregrine Falcon Population in Northwestern Mexico, 1976–77. Typewritten report by Chihuahuan Desert Research Institute, Contribution no. 40.

Hubbard, John P. 1969. The Relationships and Evolution of the *Dendroica coronata* Complex. *Auk* 86:393–432.

Hunt, W. Grainger. 1974. The Significance of Wilderness Ecosystems in Western Texas and Adjacent Regions in the Ecology of the Peregrine. In: *Transactions of the Symposium on the Biological Resources of the Chihuahuan Desert Region, U.S. and Mexico*. U.S. Department of the Interior, National Park Service, Transactions and Proceedings Series, no. 3:609–616.

———. 1975. The Chihuahuan Desert Peregrine Falcon Survey, 1975. Typewritten report to National Park Service.

———. 1976*a*. Peregrine Falcons in West Texas: Results of the 1976 Nesting Survey. Mimeographed report to Texas Parks and Wildlife Department.

———. 1976*b*. The Peregrine Population in the Chihuahuan Desert and Surrounding Mountain Ranges: An Evaluation Through 1976. Typewritten report to National Park Service.

Johnson, Brenda S. 1976. Continuing Studies of Raptors in Two National Parks in Western Texas, 1976. Typewritten report to National Park Service.

———, and W. G. Hunt. 1977. DDT and the Diet of Texas Peregrine Falcons. Report to National Park Service by Chihuahuan Desert Research Institute.

Key, J. J. 1980. Peregrine Falcon Breeding Status in Texas National Parks, 1980. Chihuahuan Desert Research Institute, Contribution no. 97.

Kowaleski, C. T., and V. R. Wade. 1977. Texas Peregrine Eyrie Search, 1977. Typewritten report to National Park Service by Chihuahuan Desert Research Institute.

Kuban, Joe F., Jr. 1977. The Ecological Organization of Hummingbirds in the Chisos Mountains, Big Bend National Park, Texas. M.A. thesis, University of Texas at Arlington.

McBee, Lena G., and Mary Belle Keefer. 1967. Field Checklist of Birds—Region of El Paso, Texas. El Paso Audubon Society.

Marshall, Joe T., Jr. 1967. *Parallel Variation in North and Middle American Screech Owls*. Los Angeles, CA: Monographs of the Western Foundation of Vertebrate Zoology.

Martin, Robert F. 1974. Syntopic Culvert Nesting of Cave and Barn Swallows in Texas. *Auk* 91:776–782.

Maxon, George E. 1916*a*. Military Oologing in Texas. *Oologist* 33(10):172–173.

———. 1916*b*. A Soldier Ornithologist. *Oologist* 33(12): 205–206.

Miller, Alden H. 1955. The Avifauna of the Sierra del Carmen of Coahuila, Mexico. *Condor* 57:154–178.

Miller, Jody and Clay. 1970. List of Birds Seen on the Miller Ranch. Typewritten list.

Montgomery, Thomas H., Jr. 1905. Summer Resident Birds of Brewster County, Texas. *Auk* 22:12–15.

Neill, R. L., and T. M. Allen. 1979. Concentrated Avian Utilization of an Early Flowering Century Plant (*Agave havardiana*). In: *Proceedings of the First Conference on Scientific Research in the National Parks, Vol. 1*. U.S. Department of the Interior, National Park Service, Transactions and Proceedings Series, no. 5:475–478.

Nelson, Richard Clay. 1970. An Additional Nesting Record of the Lucifer Hummingbird in the United States. *Southwestern Naturalist* 15:135–136.

Oberholser, Harry C. 1902. Some Notes from Western Texas. *Auk* 19:300–301.

———. 1974. *The Bird Life of Texas*. Austin: University of Texas Press.

Ohlendorf, Harry F., and Robert F. Patton. 1971. Nesting Record of Mexican Duck (*Anas diazi*) in Texas. *Wilson Bulletin* 83:97.

Palmer, Ralph S. 1962. *Handbook of North American Birds, Vol. 1*. New Haven, CT: Yale University Press.

Parker, K. C. 1982. The Structure of Bird Communities in North American Deserts. Ph.D. dissertation, University of Wisconsin, Madison.

Peterson, Roger Tory. 1960. *A Field Guide to the Birds of Texas*. Boston: Houghton-Mifflin.

———, and Edward L. Chalif. 1973. *A Field Guide to Mexican Birds*. Boston: Houghton-Mifflin.

Phillips, Allan R. 1968. The Instability of the Distribution of Land Birds in the Southwest. *Papers of the Archeological Society of New Mexico* 1:129–162.

———, Joe Marshall, and Gale Monson. 1964. *The Birds of Arizona*. Tucson: University of Arizona Press.

Pulich, Warren M., Sr., and Warren M. Pulich, Jr. 1963. The Nesting of the Lucifer Hummingbird in the United States. *Auk* 80: 370–371.

Quillin, Roy W. 1935. New Bird Records from Texas. *Auk* 52: 324–325.

Raitt, Ralph J. 1967. Relationship Between Black-eared and Plain-eared Forms of Bushtits (*Psaltriparus*). *Auk* 84:503–528.

Robinson, S. M. 1973. Ethological Study of *Vermivora crissalis* in the Chisos Mountains, Texas. M.S. thesis, Sul Ross State University, Alpine, TX.

Rooney, Walter. 1966. Interview taped by Doug Evans for National Park Service.

Scott, Peter E. 1978. The Last Five Years at Big Bend. Talk presented to the Texas Ornithological Society, May 18.

———. 1979. Peregrine Falcon Observations in Big Bend NP in 1979. Typewritten report to National Park Service.

Smith, Austin Paul. 1917. Some Birds of the Davis Mountains, Texas. *Condor* 19:161–165.

Smith, Tarleton F. 1936. Wildlife Report on the Proposed Big Bend National Park of Texas. Typewritten report to National Park Service, October 11.

Sprunt, Alexander, Jr. 1950. The Colima Warbler of the Big Bend. *Audubon Magazine* 52:84–91.

Stevenson, John O. 1935. General Wildlife Considerations of the Big Bend Area of Texas. Typewritten report to National Park Service.

———, and Tarleton F. Smith. 1938. Additions to the Brewster County, Texas, Bird List. *Condor* 40:184.

Stine, Doug. 1966. The Birds of Balmorhea Lake. Typewritten report, Sul Ross State College, Alpine, TX, May 10.

Sutton, George M. 1935. An Expedition to the Big Bend Country. *The Cardinal* 4:107.

———. 1936. *Birds in the Wilderness*. New York: Macmillan Co.

———. 1951. *Mexican Birds—First Impressions*. Norman: University of Oklahoma Press.

———, and Josselyn Van Tyne. 1935. A New Red-tailed Hawk from Texas. Occasional Papers, Museum of Zoology, University of Michigan, no. 321, September 23.

Taylor, Walter P., W. B. McDougall, and W. B. Davis. 1944. Preliminary Report of an Ecological Survey of Big Bend National Park. Mimeographed report to National Park Service, March–June.

Thompson, Ben H. 1934. Report upon the Wildlife of the Big Bend Area of the Rio Grande, Texas. Typewritten report to National Park Service, April 18.

Thompson, William Lay. 1953. The Ecological Distribution of the Birds of the Black Gap Area, Brewster County, Texas. *Texas Journal of Science* 2:158–177.

Van Tyne, Josselyn. 1929. Notes on Some Birds of the Chisos Mountains of Texas. *Auk* 46:204–206.

———. 1936. The Discovery of the Nest of the Colima Warbler (*Vermivora crissalis*). Miscellaneous Publications, University of Michigan, no. 33.

———, and George M. Sutton. 1937. The Birds of Brewster County, Texas. Miscellaneous Publications, University of Michigan, no. 37.

Wauer, Roland H. 1967*a*. Report on the Colima Warbler Census. Mimeographed report to National Park Service, May 29.

———. 1967*b*. Winter and Early Spring Birds in Big Bend. *Bulletin of the Texas Ornithological Society* 1(1):8.

———. 1967*c*. Further Evidence of Bushtit Lumping in Texas. *Bulletin of the Texas Ornithological Society* 1(5–6):1.

———. 1967*d*. Colima Warbler Census in Big Bend's Chisos Mountains. *National Parks Magazine* 41:8–10.

———. 1967e. First Thick-billed Kingbird Record for Texas. *Southwestern Naturalist* 12:485–486.

———. 1968*a*. *Checklist of the Birds of Big Bend National Park*. Big Bend National Park, TX: Big Bend Natural History Association.

———. 1968*b*. The Groove-billed Ani in Texas. *Southwestern Naturalist* 13:452.

———. 1969*a*. Hummingbirds of the Big Bend. *Bulletin of the Texas Ornithological Society* 3:18.

———. 1969*b*. Winter Bird Records from the Chisos Mountains and Vicinity. *Southwestern Naturalist* 14:252–254.

———. 1969*c*. The History of Land Use and Some Ecological Implications, Big Bend National Park, TX. Typewritten report to National Park Service, November 25.

———. 1970*a*. Upland Plover at Big Bend National Park, Texas. *Southwestern Naturalist* 14:361–362.

———. 1970*b*. The Occurrence of the Black-vented Oriole, *Icterus wagleri*, in the United States. *Auk* 82:811–812.

———. 1971*a*. A Second Swallow-tailed Kite Record for Trans-Pecos Texas. *Wilson Bulletin* 82:462.

———. 1971*b*. Ecological Distribution of Birds of the Chisos Mountains, Texas. *Southwestern Naturalist* 16:1–29.

———. 1973*a*. Status of Certain Parulids of West Texas. *Southwestern Naturalist* 18:105–110.

———. 1973*b*. *Naturalist's Big Bend*. Santa Fe, NM: Peregrine Productions.

———. 1973*c*. Bronzed Cowbird Extends Range into the Texas Big Bend Country. *Wilson Bulletin* 85:343–344.

———. 1973*d*. Report on Harlequin Quail Release, Big Bend National Park, Texas. Typewritten report to National Park Service.

———. 1977*a*. Significance of Rio Grande Riparian Systems upon the Avifauna. In: *Importance, Preservation, and Management of Riparian Habitat: A Symposium*. U.S. Department of Agriculture, Forest Service, General Technical Report RM-43:165–174.

———. 1977*b*. Changes in the Breeding Avifauna Within the Chisos Mountains System. In: *Transactions of the Symposium on the Biological Resources of the Chihuahuan Desert Region, U.S. and Mexico*. U.S. Department of the Interior, National Park Service, Transactions and Proceedings Series, no. 3:597–608.

———. 1977*c*. Interrelations Between a Harris' Hawk and Badger. *Western Birds* 8:155.

———. 1979. Colima Warbler Status at Big Bend National Park, Texas. In: *Proceedings of the First Conference on Scientific Research in the National Parks*. U.S. Department of the Interior, National Park Service, Transactions and Proceedings Series, no. 5:474–496.

———, and Donald G. Davis. 1972. Cave Swallows in Big Bend National Park, Texas. *Condor* 74:482.

———, and J. David Ligon. 1977. Distributional Relations of Breeding Avifauna of Four Southwestern Mountain Ranges. In: *Transactions of the Symposium on the Biological Resources of the Chihuahuan Desert Region, U.S. and Mexico*. U.S. Department of the Interior, National Park Service, Transactions and Proceedings Series, no. 3:567–578.

———, and M. K. Rylander. 1968. Anna's Hummingbird in West Texas. *Auk* 85:501.

———, and James F. Scudday. 1972. Occurrence and Status of Certain Charadriiformes in the Texas Big Bend Country. *Southwestern Naturalist* 17:210–211.

Whitson, Martha A. 1971. Field and Laboratory Investigation of the Ethology of Courtship and Copulation in the Greater Roadrunner. Ph.D. dissertation, University of Oklahoma, Norman.

Wolf, David E. 1978. First Record of an Aztec Thrush in the United States. *American Birds* 32:156–157.

Wolf, Col. L. R. 1956. *Checklist of the Birds of Texas*. Kerrville, TX: personal publication.